How to read

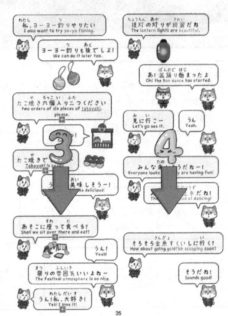

シバくん！桜もう見に行った？
Shiba-kun, have you already gone to see the cherry blossoms?

ところで夏休みの予定はもう立てた？
By the way, have you made plans for the summer vacation already?

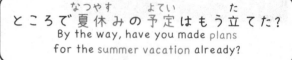

先週上野公園に行ってきたんだ
I went to Ueno Park last week.

桜が本当に素晴らしかったよ
The cherry blossoms were truly amazing.

まだだけど海に行く予定なんだ
Not yet, but I'm planning to go to the beach.

シバくんは？
How about you, Shiba-kun?

来週は雨の予報みたいだね
It looks like there's rain in the forecast next week.

北海道に旅行する予定なんだ
I'm planning a trip to Hokkaido.

花見に影響しないといいね
I hope it doesn't affect hanami (flower viewing).

願うしかないね
We can only hope.

いいアイディアだね
That's a great idea.

私もいつか北海道に行きたいな
I want to visit Hokkaido someday too.

何月に行くの？
What month are you going?

北海道は冬にも行ってみたいな
I want to visit Hokkaido in winter too.

七月だよ。六月は梅雨だしね
July. June is the rainy season, you know.

冬、すごく寒いよー
Winter there is extremely cold.

そうだね
Right.

たくさんの雪を見たいんだ
I want to see a lot of snow.

七月なら花火大会もやってるんじゃない？
In July, they might have a fireworks festival, right?

うん！やってるかもね
Yeah, There might be some.

どの季節が一番好き？
Which season do you like the most?

秋が好き
I like autumn.

花火を見ると夏を感じるよね
Watching fireworks really makes it feel like summer, doesn't it?

涼しくて、紅葉が綺麗だから
Because it's cool and the autumn leaves are beautiful.

うん！花火見れるといいなー
Yeah it does,
I hope I get to see some fireworks.

うんうん
I agree.

5

本日はツアーに参加いただきありがとうございます
Thank you for joining our tour today.

京都の美しい名所を訪れる予定です
We will be visiting the beautiful landmarks of Kyoto.

それは素晴らしいですね
That's wonderful.

初めの行き先は金閣寺でございます
Our first destination is Kinkaku-ji, the Gold Temple.

金閣寺に着きました
We have arrived at Kinkaku-ji.

金閣寺にはどんな歴史がありますか?
What is the history of Kinkaku-ji?

どのくらい滞在しますか?
How long will we stay?

約一時間です
We'll stay about one hour.

金閣寺は室町時代に建てられた仏教寺院です
Kinkaku-ji is a Buddhist temple that was built during the Muromachi period.

美しい金箔が使われていることで有名です
It's famous for the beautiful gold leaf used.

みなさんどうでしたか？
How was it everyone?

春には桜が咲き誇り、
In spring, cherry blossoms are in full bloom,

秋は紅葉が美しいです
and In autumn, autumn leaves are beautiful.

素晴らしいお寺でした！
It was an amazing temple!

でも、どの季節でも魅力があります
However, it is attractive in every season.

続いて清水寺に向かいます
We are heading to Kiyomizu Temple next.

昼食は和食のレストランに行きます
We will go to a Japanese restaurant for lunch.

京都の伝統的な料理を楽しんでいただけます
You will enjoy traditional Kyoto cuisine.

清水寺は有名ですよね
Kiyomizu Temple is famous, right?

それは楽しみです
I'm looking forward to that!

清水寺は木製の舞台が有名です
Yes, it's famous for its wooden stage.

京都市のシンボルとされています
It's considered a symbol of Kyoto city.

皆さんここから自由時間です
You all have some free time now.

また、美しい庭園もあります
There is also a beautiful garden there.

一時間後
In one hour

またここで集合しましょう
Let's meet back here.

どの季節に来るのが一番美しいですか？
What season is the most beautiful here?

たくさん写真を撮りたいです
I want to take lots of photos.

7

こんにちは
Hello.

パスポートを見せていただけますか？
May I see your passport.

チェックインしたいのですが・・・
I'd like to check in.

こちらが搭乗券です
Here is your boarding pass.

搭乗口はA30番です
The boarding gate is A number 30.

預ける荷物はいくつですか？
How many baggage do you have?

二つです
Two.

九時十分までには搭乗口までお越しください
Please come to the boarding gate before 9:10.

これは機内に持ち込めますか？
Can I bring this on board?

はい、わかりました
Yes, understood.

それはダメです
That's not allowed.

ありがとうございます
Thank you.

8

日本に来るのは初めてですか？
Is this first time visit to Japan?

両替所はどこですか？
Where is the currency exchange counter ?

どこに滞在しますか？
Where are you going to stay?

円に両替をお願いします
I'd like to exchange to yen.

キャットホテルに滞在します
I'm going to stay at Cat hotel.

ポケットの中身を出してください
Please empty your pockets.

入国の目的は何ですか？
What's the purpose of your visit?

これは持ち込めません
You can not carry this in.

観光で来ました
I'm here for sightseeing.

飛行機が遅れています
The airplane is delayed.

二週間です
For two weeks.

飛行機が欠航しています
The flight has been canceled.

窓側の席をお願いします
I'd like a window seat please.

フライトは時間通りですか？
Is the flight on time?

通路側の席をお願いします
I'd like an aisle seat please.

最終目的地はどこですか？
Where is your final destination?

9

いらっしゃいませ
Welcome.

はい
Sure.

よやく
予約してますサイです
I have a reservation
under the name Sai.

ようし　きにゅう　ねが
こちらの用紙にご記入をお願いいたします
Please fill out this form.

ありがとうございます
Thank you very much.

はい
Yes.

ありがとうございます
Thank you very much.

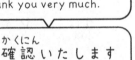
かくにん
確認いたします
Let me check.

いっぱく　よやく　　さま
一泊でご予約のサイ様ですね
You have a reservation for one night,
Sai-sama.

はい
Yes.

こちらがお部屋のカードキーです
Here is your room key card.

へや　　　　　うみ　みわた
お部屋からは海が見渡せます
From your room, you'll have a view of the sea.

ねが
パスポートをお願いいたします
May I have your passport, please?

10

あちらのエレベーターで二十二階にお進みください
Please take the elevator over there to the 22nd floor.

ありがとうございます
Thank you very much.

チェックアウトは何時ですか？
What time is checkout?

十一時です
It's at 11 a.m..

無料WIFIがご利用いただけます
You can use free WiFi.

パスワードはこちらです
Here's the password.

ありがとうございます
Thank you.

朝食はラウンジで提供しております
Breakfast is served in the lounge.

何かお困りごとや
If you need assistance or

ラウンジは何階ですか？
What floor is the lounge on?

ご質問がありましたら
any questions,

いつでもフロントまでお尋ねください
please don't hesitate to contact the front desk.

三階でございます
It's on the third floor.

ありがとうございます
Thank you.

11

スーツケースを預かってもらえますか？
Could you keep my luggage?

チェックイン、お願いします
Check-in, please.

インターネットで予約しました
I made a reservation online.

チェックアウト、お願いします
Check-out, please.

予約番号を確認してもよろしいでしょうか？
Can I confirm the reservation number?

部屋が寒いです
The room is cold.

部屋にセーフティボックスはありますか？
Is there a safe in the room?

入ってもよろしいですか？
May I come in?

タクシーを呼んでいただけますか？
Could you call a taxi for me?

タオルがありませんでした
There were no towels.

荷物をお部屋までお持ちいたします
I will bring your luggage to your room.

こちらへどうぞ
This way, please.

ごゆっくりおくつろぎください
Please make yourself comfortable.

お部屋までご案内します
Let me guide you to your room.

大浴場は何階ですか？
What floor is the large bath on?

ここで靴を脱いでください
Please take off your shoes here.

部屋に忘れ物をしました
I left something in my room.

気をつけてお帰りください
Have a safe trip to your home.

12

こんにちは
Hello

うんてんめんきょしょう　も
運転免許証はお持ちでしょうか？
Do you have your driver's license?

くるま　か
車を借りたいんですが
I'd like to rent a car.

はい
Yes, here.

よやく
ご予約はいただいておりますでしょうか？
Do you have a reservation?

てつづ　お
手続きが終わりましたら、
Once the paperwork is done,

よやく
いいえ、予約はしていません
No, I don't have a reservation.

くるま　かぎ　わた
車の鍵をお渡しします
I'll give you the car keys.

かしこまりました
I understood

はい
Yes.

くるま　さが
どのタイプの車をお探しですか？
What type of car are you looking for?

ちゅうしゃじょう　ま
駐車場でお待ちください
Please wait in the parking area.

くるま　も
車をお持ちいたします
I'll bring the car to you.

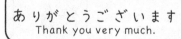

ねが
コンパクトカーをお願いします
I'd like a compact car, please.

ありがとうございます
Thank you very much.

わ
分かりました
Understood.

13

今日はハイキング行くよ
Today, we're going hiking.

季節が違うと見る景色も違うよ
The scenery looks different in each season.

うん!楽しみー
Yep, I'm so excited.

うん!ワクワクする!
Yeah, it's exciting.

ここ前にも来たんだよ
You've been here before.

よしっ!登ろう!
Alright! Let's climb!

覚えてる?
Remember?

えっ!いつ?
Huh! When?

もうすぐ展望台だよ
We're almost at the viewpoint.

春だよ!
It was in spring.

ヤッター!
Yay!

あっ!桜見たよね
Oh, right! We saw cherry blossoms.

お腹すいたー
I'm getting hungry.

そうそう
Exactly.

14

てんぼうだい　た
展望台で食べよう
Let's eat at the viewpoint.

うん
Yeah.

うん、美味しい
Yes, it's delicious.

ちゃ
お茶ある?
Do you have some tea?

つ
着いたよー
We've arrived!

のどかわ
喉渇いた
I'm thirsty.

うん、あるよ
Yep, I do.

わーすごい!
Wow, it's amazing!

はい
Here you go.

こうよう　　　　きれい
紅葉がすごく綺麗だね
The autumn leaves are incredibly beautiful.

ありがとう
Thanks!

かんどう
うん、感動する
Yeah, it's so impressive.

せんべい　た
煎餅、食べる?
Do you want to eat Senbei?

そうだね
Indeed.

た
うん、食べるー
Yes, I'll eat.

けしき　み　　　　　　べんとう
この景色を見ながらのお弁当は
Having lunch with this view,

いちだん　　　おい
一段と美味しいね
makes it even more delicious.

15

すみません
Excuse me.

きょうとえき
京都駅はどこですか?
Where is Kyoto station?

おおさか　　　　きっぷ　か
大阪までの切符を買いたいです
I'd like to buy a ticket to Osaka.

けんばいき
この券売機で
on this ticket vending machine,

つぎ　みち　みぎ　ま
次の道を右に曲がってください
Please turn right at the next street.

おおさか　　　　きんがく　えら
大阪までの金額を選んでください
Please select the fare for Osaka.

ごふん　　　　　　　　ある
それから五分くらいまっすぐ歩くと
Then, walk straight for about five minutes,

えき　つ
駅に着きます
you'll reach the station.

いくらですか?
How much is it?

ありがとうございます
Thank you.

うーんと、５８０円です
Let me see, it's 580 yen.

こま
お困りですか?
Do you need help?

ありがとうございます
Thank you.

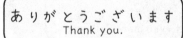

16

おおさか い
大阪に行くにはどうしたらいいですか?
How do I get to Osaka?

ひだり
ここを左にいくと
If you go left here,

ばんせん　　はっしゃ
2番線から発車しています
The trains depart from platform 2.

みどうすじせん
御堂筋線があります
you'll find the Midousuji Line.

くじじゅうごふんはつ　しんかいそく　　の
九時十五分発の新快速に乗ってください
Please take the rapid train at 9:15.

じゅうごふん　　　　　　つ
十五分くらいで着きます
You'll arrive in about 15 minutes.

なんば い　　　　でんしゃ の
そこで難波行きの電車に乗ってください
Take the train bound for Namba there.

わかりました
Got it.

ありがとうございます
Thank you.

はぁ、やっと着いたー
Phew, Finally I've arrived.

おおさか つ
大阪に着いたー
I've arrived in Osaka.

すみません
Excuse me.

つぎ ちかてつ　の
次は地下鉄に乗らないと・・・
Now I need to take the subway...

ばし
えびす橋はどこですか?
Where is Ebisu Bridge?

しょうてんがい　　　　　　　みなみ ある　　つ
この商店街をまっすぐ南に歩くと着きますよ
If you walk straight south through
this shopping street, you'll get there.

すみません
Excuse me.

しんさいばし い
心斎橋に行きたいのですが
I'd like to go to Shinsaibashi.

ありがとうございます
Thank you very much.

でんしゃ　おおさかほうめん　い
この電車は大阪方面に行きますか？
Does this train go to Osaka direction?

みなみぐち
南口はどこですか？
Where is the south exit?

きょうとえき　　の　　か
京都駅で乗り換えてください
Please transfer at Kyoto station.

きたぐち
北口はどこですか？
Where is the north exit?

かいさつ　　む
改札は向こうにあります
The ticket gate is over there.

しんかんせん　　　　　　　　　　　　　　か
新幹線のチケットはどこで買えますか？
Where can I buy Shinkansen tickets?

でんしゃ　　の
電車に乗ります
I'm getting on the train.

でんしゃ　　　　　　　きょうとえき　とうちゃく
この電車はまもなく京都駅に到着します
This train will arrive at Kyoto station shortly.

でんしゃ　　お
電車から降ります
I'm getting off the train.

じょうしゃけん　　　　も
乗車券をお持ちですか？
Do you have a ticket?

でんしゃ　とうきょうい
この電車は東京行きです
This train is bound for Tokyo.

でんしゃ　きょうと　　と
この電車は京都に止まりますか？
Does this train stop in Kyoto?

あんないじょ
案内所はどこですか？
Where is the information center?

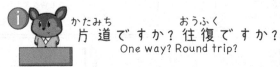

かたみち　　　　　　おうふく
片道ですか？往復ですか？
One way? Round trip?

でんしゃ　じゅうじ　しゅっぱつ
この電車は十時に出発します
This train departs at ten o'clock.

きっぷ
切符をなくしました
I lost my ticket.

早くしないと乗り遅れちゃうよ
Hurry up, or we'll miss it!

あっちだ
It's that way!

うん、わかってる
Yeah, I know

走ろう！
Let's run!

何分発？
What time does it depart?

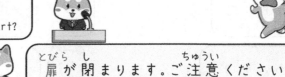

扉が閉まります。ご注意ください
The doors are closing, please be careful.

十五分発
It departs at 15.

あと一分じゃん！
Just 1 minute left!

ふー間に合ったー
Phew, we made it!

何番線？
Which platform?

よかったねー
That was close!

えーっと、二番線
Uh, platform 2.

次はカッパ駅にとまります
Next stop is Kappa Station.

えっ！反対方向じゃん！
What! It's the wrong direction!

こんにちは
Hello.

こんにちは
Hello.

とうきょう　き
東京から来ました
I'm from Tokyo.

そうなんですね
I see.

はじめまして
Nice to meet you.

ペンギンさんは?
And you, Penguin-san?

ぼく
僕はシバです
I'm Shiba.

ぼく　ほっかいどう　き
僕は北海道から来ました
I'm from Hokkaido.

ペンギンです
I'm Penguin.

ねが
よろしくお願いします
Nice to meet you.

しごと　なに
お仕事は何をされていますか?
What do you do for a living?

こちらこそ
Likewise.

すいぞくかん　はたら
水族館で働いています
I work at aquarium.

どこから来ましたか?
Where are you from?

そうですか
I see.

20

何をすることが好きですか？
What do you like to do ?

おすすめの場所はありますか？
Do you have any recommended places to visit?

今、キャンプにハマっています
I'm currently into camping.

北海道もいいですよ
Hokkaido is great too.

ペンギンさんは？
How about you, Penguin-san ?

食べ物がおいしくて
The food is delicious, and

自然もたくさんあります
there is also a lot of nature.

趣味は旅行です
My hobby is traveling.

行ってみたい
I'd like to go there.

旅行いいですね
Traveling sounds nice

最近どこに行きましたか？
Where have you been recently?

はい、行ってみてください
Yes, You should definitely visit.

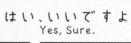

山梨に行きました
I went to Yamanashi.

連絡先を交換しませんか？
Would you like to exchange contact information?

富士山は見えましたか？
Did you see Mount Fuji ?

はい、いいですよ
Yes, Sure.

ありがとうございます
Thank you very much.

はい、とても綺麗に見えましたよ
Yes, I could see it very beautifully.

21

presentation
polite

しゅっしん
出身はどちらですか?
Where are you from ?

わたし　なまえ
私の名前はシバです
My name is Shiba.

きょうと　す
京都に住んでいます
I live in Kyoto.

にじゅうろくさい
二十六歳です
I'm 26 years old.

ね　す
寝ることが好きです
I like sleeping.

じゅうしょ
住所は〜です
My home address is〜.

りょうり　とくい
料理が得意です
I'm good at cooking.

でんわばんごう
電話番号は〜です
My phone number is〜.

すうがく　にがて
数学が苦手です
I'm not good at math.

けつえきがた　がた
血液型は〜型です
My blood type is 〜.

じゅうどう　なら
柔道を習っています
I'm learning Judo.

メールアドレスは〜です
My email address is〜.

びょういん　つと
病院に勤めています
I work at hospital.

す　た　もの
好きな食べ物は〜です
My favorite food is〜.

しゅみ　なん
趣味は何ですか?
What is your hobby?

せいねんがっぴ　ねん　がつ　にち
生年月日は〜年〜月〜日です
My date of birth is 〜year,〜month,〜day.

しゅっしん
出身はどこ？
Where are you from ?

なまえ
名前はシバだよ
My name is Shiba.

きょうと　す
京都に住んでるよ
I live in Kyoto.

にじゅうろくさい
二十六歳だよ
I'm 26 years old.

ね　　　　す
寝るのが好きなんだ
I like sleeping.

じゅうしょ
住所は～だよ
My home address is～.

りょうり　　とくい
料理が得意なんだ
I'm good at cooking.

でんわばんごう
電話番号は～だよ
My phone number is～.

すうがく　にがて
数学が苦手なんだ
I'm not good at math.

けつえきがた　　がた
血液型は～型だよ
My blood type is type～.

じゅうどう　なら
柔道を習ってるんだ
I'm learning Judo.

メールアドレスは～だよ
My email address is～.

びょういん　はたら
病院で働いてるよ
I work at hospital.

す　　　た　もの
好きな食べ物は～だよ
My favorite food is～.

しゅみ　　なに
趣味は何？
What is your hobby?

せいねんがっぴ　　ねん　がつ　にち
生年月日は～年～月～日だよ
My date of birth is ～year,～month,～day.

23

presentation

となり せき
隣の席だね
You're sitting next to me.

これからよろしく
Nice to meet you

こちらこそよろしく
Nice to meet you too.

はな
あまり話したことなかったよね
We haven't really talked much, have we?

あまりないね
No, not really.

ところで
By the way

くん しゅっしん
ゴリラ君どこの出身だっけ?
Where are you from, Gorilla-kun?

う
生まれはジャングルだよ
I was born in the Jungle.

いま きょうと す
でも今は京都に住んでるよ
But I'm currently living in Kyoto.

いま す
たぬきくんは今どこに住んでるの?
Where do you live now Tanuki-kun?

いまこうべ す
今神戸に住んでるよ
I currently live in Kobe.

そうなんだ
I see.

やす ひ なに
休みの日は何してるの?
What do you do on your days off?

ね
うーん、寝てる
Hmm, mostly just sleep.

しゅみ
趣味は?
Any hobbies?

24

そうだね一、柔道を習ってるよ
Well, I take lessons in judo,

それと、料理が得意かな
and I'm good at cooking, I think

へーそうなんだ！
Oh, that's great!

来週？
Next week?

わかった！来週約束ね！
Alright, it's a plan for next week then.

うん
Yeah.

今度、うちに食べにおいでよ
How about coming over to my place to eat sometime?

もう行かなきゃ
I've gotta go now.

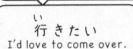

うん、じゃあまた来週
Yeah, see you next week.

え！いいの？
Really? Is that okay?

行きたい
I'd love to come over.

いつ行っていい？
When can I come?

バイバイ
Bye

またね
See you later

えっ！また今度
Eh! another time.

また今度っていつ？
When is "another time"?

何作ろうかな・・・
I wonder what should I make...

ゴリラくんずっとバナナ食べてたし
Gorilla-kun was eating bananas all the time,

バナナケーキでも作ろうかな・・・
so maybe I'll make a banana cake...

・・・

25

Greeting polite

おはようございます
Good morning.

こんにちは
Hello.

お元気ですか？
(げんき)
How are you ?

こんばんは
Good evening.

おやすみなさい
Good night.

行ってきます
(い)
I'll go now.

お久しぶりです
(ひさ)
Long time no see.

行ってらっしゃい
(い)
Have a safe trip.
This phrase is used
when someone is leaving the house.

お帰りなさい
(かえ)
Welcome home.

ただいま
I'm home.

よろしくお願いします
(ねが)
It's pleasure to meet you. / Let's keep in
touch. /Thank you in advance. / Best regards.

いただきます
This phrase is used before starting a meal to
express gratitude for the meal.

お疲れ様です
(つか さま)
This phrase is used as both a greeting at the end
of a workday and as a way to express gratitude.

ごちそうさまでした
This phrase is used when a meal is over
to thank the person who prepared it.

お先に失礼します
(さき しつれい)
Excuse me for leaving before you.
This phrase is used when you leave work before
your colleagues.

お世話になります
(せ わ)
Thank you for your support,
kindness, work, cooperation.

26

Greeting casual

おはよう
Good morning.

ちょうし
調子どう?
How is it going?

げんき
元気?
How are you ?

さいきん
最近どう?
How have you been lately?

おやすみ
Good night.

き
気をつけてね
Take care.

ひさ
久しぶり
Long time no see.

バイバイ
Good bye.

あ　うれ
会えて嬉しい
I'm glad to see you.

またね
See you later.

よろしく
It's nice to meet you. / Let's keep in touch.
/Thank you in advance.

あした
また明日
See you tomorrow.

つか
お疲れ
This phrase is used as both a greeting at the end of
a workday and as a way to express gratitude.

かえ
お帰り
Welcome home.

さき　かえ
先に帰るね
I'm going to go ahead.

あ
明けましておめでとう
Happy New Year.

27

Greeting
polite

ちょうし
調子 は どう で す か?
How is it going?

さいきん
最近 は どう で す か?
How have you been lately?

はじめまして
Nice to meet you.

ようこそ
Welcome.

いらっしゃいませ
Welcome. (at store, shop)

じゃま
お邪魔します
This phrase is used
when entering someone's house.

あ　でき　こうえい
お会い出来て光栄です
It's nice to seeing you.

さようなら
Good bye.

あ
また お会いしましょう
See you later.

あした　あ
また明日お会いしましょう
See you tomorrow.

らいしゅう　あ
また来週お会いしましょう
See you next week.

き
お気をつけて
Take care.

じゃま
お邪魔しました
This phrase is used
when leaving someone's house.

とし
よいお年を
This phrase is used to wish someone a happy
and prosperous New Year.

あ
明けましておめでとうございます
Happy New Year.

28

ヤッホー! 元気？
Hi, how are you?

日曜日はカラオケに行った
On Sunday, we went to karaoke.

おっ!シバくん
Hey! Shiba-kun.

いいねぇー
Nice

元気だよ
I'm good.

何の映画見たの？
What movie did you see?

最近どうしてた？
What have you been up to lately ?

最新のアクション映画を見たんだ
We saw the latest action movie.

仕事は忙しいけど
Work's been busy but

かなり面白かったよ
It was quite interesting.

週末は友達と遊んでたよ
I hung out with friends over the weekend.

ストレス発散できたみたいだね!
It seems like you were able to relieve stress.

土曜日は映画を見に行って、
On Saturday, we went to see a movie,

うん
Yeah.

また今度遊びに行こう
Let's hung out sometime .

うんうん!
Yeah, yeah!

29

これ は 何(なん) です か？
What is this?

どんな～です か？
What kind of ～?

あれ は 何(なん) です か？
What is that?

何故(なぜ) です か？
Why?

どうしたんです か？
What happened? / What's wrong?

いつ が いい です か？
When would you prefer ?

どう 思(おも)います か？
What do you think about it?

どっち が いい です か？
Which one would you prefer?
(Asks for a choice between two options.)

何(なに) を しています か？
What are you doing ?

どれ が いい です か？
Which one would you prefer?
(Asks for a choice among three or more options.)

トイレ は どこ です か？
Where is the restroom?

どの よう に 行(い)けば いい です か？
How do I get there?

どこ に 行(い)きます か？
Where are you going ?

どれ くらい 時間(じかん) が かかります か？
How long time does it take?

どこ に 住(す)んでいます か？
Where do you live ?

いくら です か？
How much is it?

30

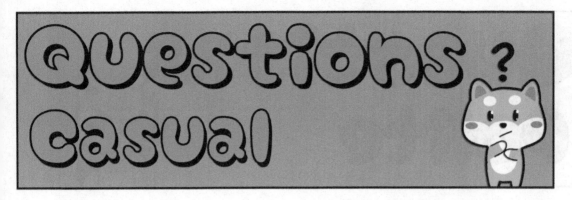

Questions ?
Casual

これ は 何(なに)？
What is this?

どんな〜？
What kind of〜?

あれ は 何(なに)？
What is that?

何(なん)で？, どうして？
Why? / How come?

どうしたの？
What happened? / What's wrong?

いつ が いい？
When is good for you ?

When?

どう 思(おも)う？
What do you think about it?

どっち が いい？
Which one do you prefer?
(Asks for a choice between two options.)

何(なに)してるの？
What are you doing?

どれ が いい？
Which one do you prefer?
(Asks for a choice among three or more options.)

トイレ は どこ？
Where is the restroom?

どうやって 行(い)けば いい？
How do I get there?

どこ に 行(い)くの？
Where are you going?

どれくらい 時間(じかん) かかる？
How long time does it take?

どこ に 住(す)んでるの？
Where do you live?

いくら？
How much is it?

31

Questions polite

何か質問はありますか？
Do you have any questions?

～はありますか？
Do you have ～?
(the existence or availability of something.)

今日は何曜日ですか？
What day is it today?

～を持っていますか？
Do you have ～?
(possession or having something at the moment.)

日本に行ったことはありますか？
Have you ever been to Japan?

どこに置けばいいですか？
Where should I put it?

分かりますか？
Do you get it? / Does it make sense?

～していただけますか？
Could you～?

知っていますか？
Do you know it?

～してもいいですか？
May I～? / Can I～? / Could I～?

書いてもらえますか？
Could you write it down?

もう少しゆっくり話していただけますか？
Could you speak more slowly?

ここに座ってもいいですか？
May I sit here?

これを使ってもいいですか？
Is it okay to use this?

写真を撮ってもらえますか？
Do you mind taking a picture of us?

これはどういう意味ですか？
What does this mean?

32

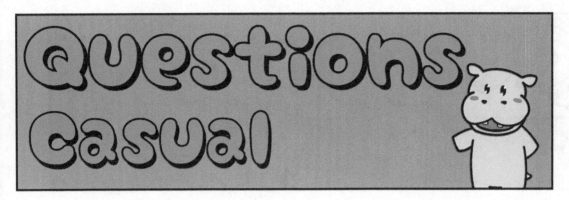

Questions Casual

なに　しつもん
何か質問はある？
Do you have any questions?

きょう　　　なんようび
今日は何曜日？
What day is it today?

にほん　い
日本に行ったことある？
Have you ever been to Japan?

わ
分かる？
Do you get it? / Does it make sense?

し
知ってる？
Do you know it?

か
書いてくれる？
Can you write it down?

すわ
ここに座ってもいい？
Can I sit here?

しゃしん　と
写真を撮ってくれる？
Can you take a picture of us?

〜はある？
Do you have 〜?
(the existence or availability of something.)

も
〜を持ってる？
Do you have 〜?
(possession or having something at the moment.)

お
どこに置けばいい？
Where should I put it?

〜してくれる？
Can you〜?

〜してもいい？
Can I〜? / Could I〜?

すこ　　　　　　　　　はな
もう少しゆっくり話してくれる？
Could you speak more slowly?

つか
これを使ってもいい？
Is it okay to use this?

いみ
これはどういう意味？
What does this mean?

33

なに
何してるの?
What are you up to?

うん
Yeah

りょこう　　　　　　　　つく
旅行のプランを作ってる
I'm making travel plans.

ひこうき
飛行機でどのくらいかかるの?
How long does it take you to get there by plane?

どこに行くの?
Oh, where are you going?

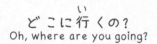

にじかん
二時間くらいかな
About two hours, I think.

おきなわ
沖縄
Okinawa.

たの
楽しみだね
Exciting!

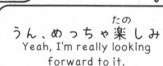

い
いつ行くの?
When are you going?

うん、めっちゃ楽しみ
Yeah, I'm really looking forward to it.

ことし　なつ
今年の夏だよ
This summer.

おきなわ　なに　　　　　よてい
沖縄で何する予定なの?
What are your plans in Okinawa?

いいね
Nice.

なつ　おきなわさいこう
夏の沖縄最高じゃん!
Okinawa in the summer is awesome!

うみ　およ　　　いちばん　もくてき
海で泳ぐのが一番の目的だよ!
the main purpose is to swim in the sea!

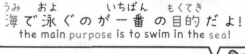

34

水着どっちがいいと思う？
Which swimsuit do you think is better?

帰ってきたら見せてね
Show them to me when you come back.

もちろん
Sure.

こっちかな
I think this one.

お土産楽しみにしてる
I'm looking forward to souvenirs.

じゃあ、こっちにする
Alright, I'll go with this one.

何か特別に欲しいものある？
Is there anything specific you want?

沖縄の海すごく綺麗だよね
Okinawa's sea is incredibly beautiful, isn't it?

ちんすこう
Chinsuko cookies.

うん、すごく綺麗だよ
Yes, it's really beautiful.

防水カメラを買ったんだ
I bought a waterproof camera.

美味しいよね！
They're delicious!

準備万端じゃん！
You're all set then.

わかった、買ってくるよ
Great, I'll bring some back for you!

海の中でたくさん写真を撮るんだ！
I'm going to take lots of photos underwater.

ヤッター
Yay!

Please
polite

しょうしょう　ま
少々お待ちください
Please wait a moment.

ねが
お願いします
Please.

てつだ
手伝ってください
Please help me.

わす
これを忘れないでください
Please don't forget this.

き
こちらに来てください
Please come here.

ほ
〜が欲しいのですが
I'd like〜.

み
これを見てください
Please look at this.

いちど
もう一度やってみてください
Please try it again.

き
これを聞いてください
Please listen to this.

えいご　おし
これを英語で教えてください
Please explain this in English.

か
ここに書いてください
Please write it here.

いちど い
もう一度言ってください
Please say it again.

し
ドアを閉めてください
Please close the door.

と
それを取ってください
Please take that. / Please pass me that.

ため
これを試してみてください
Please try this.

わたし
私は〜にします
I'll take〜. / I'll have〜.

please
casual

ちょっと待って
Wait a moment.

お願い
Please.

手伝って
Help me.

これを忘れないで
Don't forget this.

こっちに来て
Come here.

〜が欲しい
I want 〜.

これを見て
Look at this.

もう一度やってみて
Try it again.

これを聞いて
Listen to this.

これを英語で教えて
Explain this in English.

ここに書いて
Write it here.

もう一度言って
Say it again.

ドアを閉めて
Close the door.

それを取って
Take that. / Pass me that.

これを試してみて
Try this.

私は〜にする
I'll take〜. / I'll have〜.

Response Polite

ありがとうございます
Thank you very much

おそらく
Probably. / Maybe.

もう わけ
申し訳ございません / ごめんなさい
I apologise / I'm sorry.

まだです
Not yet.

はい
Yes.

どういたしまして
You're welcome.

いいえ
No.

だいじょうぶ
大丈夫です
I'm fine. / That's alright.

たし　　　　とお
確かにその通りです
That's true.

そうかもしれません
I guess so.

き
気にしないでください
Never mind. / Don't worry about it.

それでいいです
I'm ok with it.

わ
分かりました
I understood. / I got it.

そうですね
Right.

そうです
Yes, it is.

そうしましょう
Let's do that.

おも
そう思います
I think so.

なん
何でもありません
Nothing.

38

Response Casual

ありがとう
Thank you.

ごめん
I'm sorry.

うん
Yeah.

ううん
No.

確かにその通りだね
That's true.

気にしないで
Never mind. / Don't worry about it.

分かった
I got it. / I understood.

そう
Yeah, it is.

そう思う
I think so.

たぶん
Probably. / Maybe.

まだだよ
Not yet.

全然
Not at all.

大丈夫だよ
I'm fine. / That's alright.

 そうかもね
I guess so.

それでいいよ
I'm ok with it.

そうだね
Right.

そうしよう
Let's do that.

何でもないよ
Nothing.

本日はお越しいただきありがとうございます
Thank you for coming today.

それでは、始めましょう
Let's get started then.

こちらこそ、ありがとうございます
Thank you for having me.

まず抹茶を茶碗にいれてください
First, please put matcha in the tea bowl.

茶道について学ぶことが楽しみです
I'm looking forward to learning about tea ceremony.

お湯をいれてください
Pour hot water into it?

お茶室の庭園、本当に美しいですね
The tea garden here is truly beautiful.

はい
Yes

細かい泡がたつように混ぜてください
Now whisk it until fine bubbles form.

自然の美との調和が茶道の一部です
The harmony with the beauty of nature is part of tea ceremony.

できましたね
Well done.

お菓子をどうぞ
Please have some sweets.

お茶は季節や時間によって
Tea offers depending on the season and time,

違う風味が楽しめます
you can enjoy different flavor.

ありがとうございます
Thank you.

それが茶道の魅力です
and that's what makes the tea ceremony so captivating.

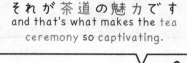

まずお辞儀をします
Let's begin with a bow.

本当に素晴らしい体験です
This is truly an incredible experience.

お辞儀は茶道の礼儀の一部ですね
Bowing is part of the etiquette in the Way of Tea ceremony.

茶道を学ぶことは
Learning the Way of Tea ceremony,

文化と自然との絶妙な調和を感じるチャンスです
gives us the chance to feel the exquisite harmony between culture and nature.

茶碗を時計方向に三回、回してください
Please rotate the tea bowl three times clockwise.

はい
Absolutely

では、いただきましょう
Now, let's enjoy the tea.

そして茶道は
and the way of tea ceremony

美味しいです
It's good.

精神的な平和と静けさをもたらします
brings a sense of spiritual peace and tranquility.

お越しいただきありがとうございます
Thank you for coming.

この柄と色が素敵ですね
This pattern and color are lovely.

今日は夏祭りの浴衣をお探しですね？
Are you looking for a yukata for the summer festival today?

はい、そうです
Yes, that's right.

はい
Yes

お似合いになると思います
I think it suits you

浴衣を着て、夏祭りを楽しみたいです
I want to enjoy the summer festival in a yukata.

こちらの浴衣でしたら
With this yukata,

こちらの帯はいかがでしょうか？
How about this obi (sash) to go with it?

まずは着る浴衣を選びましょう
First, let's choose the yukata you'd like to wear.

いいですね
That's nice.

この中からお好きな浴衣をお選びください
Please pick your favorite one from these options.

それでお願いします
I'll take it

では、着付けを始めますね
Alright, let's start with the dressing then.

きつすぎですか？
Is it too tight?

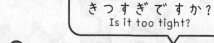

大丈夫です
It's fine.

では浴衣に着替えてください
Please change into a yukata.

最後に、髪飾りをおつけいたします
At last, I'll put on a hair accessory.

はい
Yes.

どれになさいますか？
Which one would you like？

お着替えいただけましたか？
Have you changed into your yukata?

はい、着替えました
Yes, I have changed.

この髪飾りでお願いします
I'd like this hair accessory, please

まず、浴衣の裾の長さを調整します
First, I'll adjust the length of the yukata.

どうぞ、鏡の前に立って、
Please stand in front of the mirror and

紐を結びます
I'll tie the string.

仕上がりをご確認ください
check the final look.

次に、帯を締めます
Next, I'll tie the obi.

はい、お願いします
Yes, please.

綺麗です。ありがとうございます
It looks beautiful. Thank you very much.

わー！お祭りだぁー！
Wow, it's a festival!

ネコちゃんの浴衣可愛いね
Neko-chan, your yukata looks pretty.

シバくんの甚平もかっこいいよ
Shiba-kun, your jinbei looks cool too.

ありがとう！
Thank you.

盛り上がってるねー
It's so lively here, isn't it?

うん！
Yeah!

ねぇ何食べたい？
hey what do you want to eat?

たこ焼きー
Takoyaki.

あそこにたこ焼きの屋台があったよ
There's a takoyaki stall over there.

じゃあ買いに行こっ！
Let's go buy some.

金魚すくいしてるー！
They're doing goldfish scooping.

後でやる？
Do you wanna try it later?

うん！やりたい！
Yes, I wanna do it.

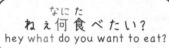

44

私、ヨーヨー釣りやりたい
I also want to try yo-yo fishing.

ヨーヨー釣りも後でしよ!
We can do it later too.

たこ焼き六個入り二つください
Two orders of six pieces of takoyaki, please.

はいよっ!
Sure!

たこ焼きできたよー
Takoyaki is ready.

うわーっ!美味しそうー!
Wow! it looks delicious!

あそこに座って食べる?
Shall we sit over there and eat?

うん!
Yeah!

祭りの雰囲気いいよねー
The festival atmosphere is so nice.

うん!私、大好き!
Yes! I love it!

提灯のあかりが綺麗だね
The lantern lights are beautiful.

あ!盆踊り始まったよ
Oh! the Bon dance has started.

見に行こー
Let's go see it.

うん
Yeah.

みんな楽しそうだねー!
Everyone looks like they are having fun!

みんな踊り上手だね!
They are so good at dancing!

そろそろ金魚すくいしに行く?
How about going goldfish scooping soon?

そうだね!
Sounds good!

あ
明けましておめでとう
Happy New Year!

ぼく ねむ ねむ
僕、眠たくて眠たくて‥
I was so sleepy,

あ
明けましておめでとう
Happy New Year!

ね た
寝てしまって食べてない
I fell asleep and didn't eat.

ことし
今年もよろしくね
Let's have a great year together.

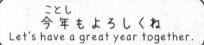

そっか
I see.

こちらこそよろしく
Same here, looking forward to it.

きょう せちりょうりた
今日はお節料理食べれるじゃん
You can have Osechi (Japanese traditional
New Year's dish) today.

ぞうに
お雑煮もね
Ozoni soup too

としこ た
年越しそば食べた?
Did you eat Toshikoshi soba?
(New Year's Eve soba)

そうだね
That's right.

しょうがつぶと
正月太りしそう
I might gain some weight
during New Year holidays.

もちろん
Of course.

シバくんは?
How about you? Shiba-kun.

わたし
たぶん私も
Yeah, I think I will too.

46

ところで、ネコちゃん初詣（はつもうでい）行く予定（よてい）なの？
By the way, Are you planning to go for Hatsumoude, Neko-chan?

うん、行（い）こうと思（おも）ってるよ
Yeah, I'm thinking of going.

一緒（いっしょ）に行（い）かない？
Want to go together?

3日（みっか）か4日（よっか）くらいかな
Maybe around the 3rd or 4th.

混雑（こんざつ）も少（すこ）しは落（お）ち着（つ）くだろうし
It should be less crowded by then.

うん、いいよ
Sure, that sounds good.

そうだね！そうしよ
That sounds like a plan!

私（わたし）、おみくじする！
I will do omikuji !

どこの神社（じんじゃ）に行（い）くつもり？
Which shrine are you planning to go?

僕（ぼく）も！
Me too!

狐神社（きつねじんじゃ）に行（い）くつもり
I'm thinking of going to the Kitsune Shrine.

お守（まも）りも買（か）いたい！
I want to buy a good luck charm too.

そっか
I see.

そうだね！
Yeah!

いつがいい？
When is good for you?

いらっしゃい
Welcome.

ハハ
Haha.

おとなふたり　こどもひとり
大人二人、子供一人です
Two adults and one child.

おんなゆ　　　　　　　　　あと
ママは女湯だからまた後でね
Mom is going to women's bath
so see you later.

えん
1,300円ね
1,300 yen in total.

うん
Yeah

はい
Yes.

ひゃくえんだまも
百円玉持ってる?
Do you have a 100 yen coin?

いちじかんご
じゃあ一時間後くらい?
So in about an hour?

ロッカーでいるかもよ
You might need it for the locker

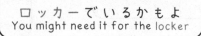

はーい
Ok.

も
持ってる
Yes I have it

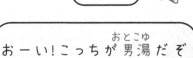

おとこゆ
おーい!こっちが男湯だぞ
Hey! The men's bath is this way.

ここの回転寿司初めてきたよ
<ruby>回転寿司<rt>かいてんずし</rt></ruby>
<ruby>初<rt>はじ</rt></ruby>
I'm here for the first time at this conveyor belt sushi place.

二名様でお待ちのネコ様
<ruby>二名様<rt>にめいさま</rt></ruby>
<ruby>待<rt>ま</rt></ruby>
<ruby>様<rt>さま</rt></ruby>
Neko-sama, we have a table ready for two.

はい、ここです
Yes, we are here.

えっ!そうなの?
Oh, are you?

こちらの席へどうぞ
<ruby>席<rt>せき</rt></ruby>
Right this way to your table.

うん
Yeah.

ありがとうございます
Thank you very much.

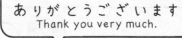
テーブルとカウンターどっちがいい?
Do you prefer a table or the counter?

何頼む?
<ruby>何頼<rt>なにたの</rt></ruby>
What do you wanna order?

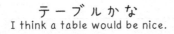
テーブルかな
I think a table would be nice.

マグロとタイとイカと海老と
<ruby>海老<rt>えび</rt></ruby>
I'll have some tuna, sea bream, squid, shrimp,

オッケー
Okay.

シメサバとサーモンと赤貝と
<ruby>赤貝<rt>あかがい</rt></ruby>
Mackerel, salmon, and red clam and...

ちょっ！ちょっと待って
Wait! give me a moment.

一気に頼みすぎでしょ！
You're ordering quite a lot all at once!

お寿司きたよ
The sushi is here.

ハハハ
Hahaha

すっごくお腹すいてるから
I'm really hungry.

あっ！またきたよ
Oh! it's here again.

急がなくても時間はあるから
No rush, we have time.

あっ！また
Whoops! it comes again.

そうだね
That's true.

一気に頼むから全部きたじゃん！
because you ordered a lot all at once,
it all came together!

とりあえずこれでお寿司来るの待とう
Let's start with this, and we'll wait for the sushi to come.

お茶いれるね
I'll make you tea.

大丈夫！全部食べるから
Don't worry I'll eat all of them.

ありがとう
Thank you.

うまーい!!!
It's so good!!!

51

こんにちは
Hello

は　　　　　　　くも
晴れたり、曇ったりと
It's sunny and cloudy at times,

はちがつ ふつか すいようび
八月二日水曜日
August 2nd, Wednesday

か　　　　　　　てんき
変わりやすい天気になりそうです
It looks like the weather will be changeable.

てんきよほう　　　　つた
天気予報をお伝えします
I'll tell you the weather forecast.

きおん たか あつ　　き
気温は高く暑さに気をつけてください
The temperature is high,
please be cautious of the heat.

にしにほん　　　　ちゅうぶ ちほう
西日本から中部地方にかけては
In western Japan to the Chubu region,

かさ　　わす　　　　　　　も
傘をお忘れなくお持ちください
Please don't forget to take an umbrella.

くも　ひろ　　あめ　ふ　　　　てんき
雲が広がり、雨の降りやすい天気になりそうです
There will be cloudy skies with a chance of rain.

しこくちほう　　　　はげ　　あめ　よそう
四国地方では、激しい雨が予想されます
In the Shikoku region, we're expecting heavy rain.

かんとうちほう　とうほくちほう
関東地方と東北地方は
Kanto region and Tohoku region ,

よ　いちにち
それではみなさん 良い一日を!
Have a great day, everyone!

52

いい天気ですね
It's good weather.

明日は台風がくるみたいですよ
It looks like a typhoon is coming tomorrow.

天気が悪いですね
It's bad weather.

風が涼しくて気持ち良いですね
The breeze is cool and pleasant.

今日は暑いですね
It's hot today.

今日は晴れてよかったですね
I'm glad it's sunny today.

昨日は寒かったですね
It was cold yesterday.

北海道は雪がたくさん降ります
Hokkaido gets a lot of snow.

傘を持っていますか?
Do you have an umbrella?

見てください! 虹が出てます
Look! There's a rainbow.

外は雨が降っていますよ
It's raining outside.

今日の気温は二十五度です
Today's temperature is 25 degrees.

空が曇ってますね
The sky is cloudy.

太陽が眩しいですね
The sun is bright.

天気予報を見ましたか?
Have you check the weather forecast?

今日は湿度が高いですね
It's very humid today.

月が綺麗ですね
The moon is beautiful.

星がキラキラ輝いていますね
The stars are shining brightly.

53

ヤッホー
Howdy

でも風が涼しくて気持ちいいね
The breeze feels cool and refreshing though.

久しぶりだね
It's been a while.

今日、天気悪いね
The weather's not looking great today, huh?

うん、最近ずっと暑かったもんね
Yeah, it's been hot for quite a while.

うわっ！雨が降ってきた！
Oh no! It's starting to rain!

空が曇ってるね
The sky is all cloudy.

とにかくどこか中に入ろう
Anyway, let's go somewhere inside.

だいぶ降ってきたね！
It's really coming down!

天気予報みた？
Did you check the weather forecast?

台風が近づいてるみたいだよ
Seems like a typhoon is approaching.

雷も鳴ってる
I hear thunder too.

そうなんだ
Oh, really.

カフェでも行こっか！
How about going to cafe?

うん、いいよ
Sure

54

台風の進路や強さを確認したほうがいいね!
We should check the typhoon's path and intensity!

ほら外見て!
Look outside!

雨落ち着いてきたよ!
The rain is calming down now!

けっこうゆっくりみたいだよ
I heard it's moving quite slowly.

あっ!本当だね
Oh, you are right.

うん、もうやみそうだね
Yeah, it looks like it's stopping.

そうなんだ
Is that so.

買い物行っとかないといけないかなぁ
I wonder if I should go grocery shopping.

急に晴れてきたよ!
It suddenly cleared up!

確かに、そうだね
Indeed, that's right.

台風近づいてるけど、
Even though the typhoon is approaching,

見て!虹が出てる!
Look! There's a rainbow!

来ないかもしれないよね
it might not actually come here, right?

うん
Yeah.

そういうのけっこうあるよね
There are situations like that sometimes.

ほんとだ!綺麗だね!
You are right! It's beautiful!

おはよー
Good morning

おはよー
Good morning

うん
Yeah

ひがさ
日傘も持ってきた?
Did you bring a sun umbrella ?

てんき
いい天気だねー
It's lovely weather today, isn't it?

うん、晴れてよかったね
Yeah, it's great that it's sunny.

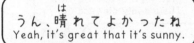

いちおうも
うん、一応持ってきた
Yeah, just in case I brought.

たいよう　まぶ
太陽が眩しいね
The sun is really bright.

きょう　　さいこうきおんさんじゅうごど
今日の最高気温三十五度みたいだよ
Today's high might reach 35 degrees.

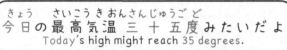

あつ
えー暑いね
Oh! That's hot.

ひがさ　　　　　　　　　　　よ
日傘をさしたほうが良さそうだね
It looks like using a sun umbrella would be a good idea.

しつど　たか
湿度も高くてジメジメしてるね
The humidity is also high, and it feels damp.

そうだね
You are right

56

寒いねー
It's cold.

うー
Ugh

今日の最低気温何度か知ってる?
Do you know today's lowest temperature?

うん、今日めっちゃ寒い
Yeah, it's incredibly cold today.

さっき天気予報みたらマイナス3度だって
I checked the weather forecast earlier,
and it said it might go down to minus 3 degrees.

えーそうなの?
Oh, seriously?

雪、降るかもしれないね
It might even snow.

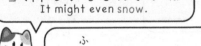 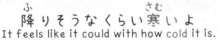

降りそうなくらい寒いよ
It feels like it could with how cold it is.

今日は早めに帰ろう
Let's plan to head home early today.

そうだね
Right

冬が近づいてる感じするね
I can sense winter approaching.

こたつに入ってゆっくりしたい
I just want to get under the kotatsu and relax.

うん
Yeah.

57

今は何時ですか？
What time is it now?

バス来ないですね・・・
The bus isn't coming, is it?

今十時十分ですよ
It's 10:10 right now.

ありがとうございます
Thank you.

タクシーで行ったほうがいいかも・・
Maybe it's better to take a taxi.

次のバスは何分に来ますか？
What time (minutes) is
the next bus coming?

どちらへ行かれるんですか？
Where are you heading to?

駅まで
to the train station.

十五分に来るはずなんですが
It should be here at fifteen, but...

ちょっと遅れてるみたいですね
It seems like it's running a little late.

じゃあ一緒に行きませんか？
Why don't we go together?

そうみたいですね
Yes, it looks that way.

そうしましょう
That sounds like a plan.

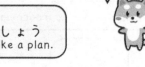

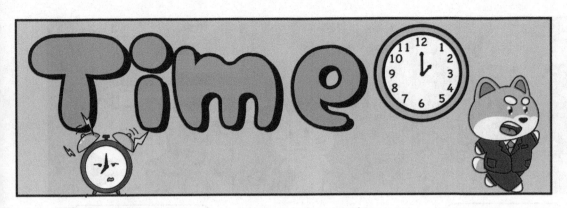

きょう なんようび
今日は何曜日ですか？
What day is it today?

あした あ
明日は空いていますか？
Are you free tomorrow?

いま なんじ
今は何時ですか？
What time is it now?

いま じ はん
今は１０時半です
It's ten thirty.

いま じ ふんまえ
今は１０時１５分前です
It's quarter to ten.

きょう ひづけ ねん がつ にち
今日の日付は、２０２３年４月１５日です
Today's date is April 15, 2023.

ごぜんちゅういそが
午前中は忙しいです
I'm busy in the morning.

ごご ひま
午後は暇です
I'm free in the afternoon.

きのう あさ
昨日の朝ヨガをしました
I did yoga yesterday morning.

ともだち い
友達とランチに行きます
I go out to lunch with friends.

きょねん き
去年もここに来ました
I came here last year too.

らいしゅう しごと いそが
来週は仕事が忙しい
I'm busy at work next week.

しゅうまつ よてい なん
週末の予定は何ですか？
What are your plans for the weekend?

せんげつ かいぎ おお
先月は会議が多かったです
I had a lot of meetings last month.

たんじょうび
誕生日はいつですか？
When is your birthday?

らいねん りょこう い
来年はたくさん旅行に行きたいです
I want to travel a lot next year.

にほん なつ む あつ
日本の夏は蒸し暑いですね
Japanese summers are hot and humid.

あき た もの おい きせつ
秋は食べ物が美味しい季節ですね
Autumn is the season for good food.

今日は何曜日？
What day is it today?

確か九時から
I think it's at 9.

今日は、木曜日だよ
It's Thursday today.

朝の？
In the morning?

あっ！そっか
Oh, right.

うん
Yeah

午前中は忙しいんだ
I'll be busy in the morning.

あのさぁ、土曜日空いてる？
Hey, are you free on Saturday?

午後から暇？
Are you free in the afternoon?

土曜日、シカちゃんと映画に行くんだ
I'm going to the movies with Shika-chan on Saturday.

うん、空いてるよ
Yeah, I'm free in the afternoon.

一緒に来る？
Do you want to come with us?

何時に待ち合わせする？
What time are we going to meet up?

何時から？
What time?

一時は？
How about 1 p.m.?

オッケー
Okay.

60

ことし
今年もあっという間だったねー
This year went by so quickly.

ほんとう　じかん　　す　　　　はや
本当、時間が過ぎるの早いよ
Yeah, time really flies.

ことし　　　　　　　いそが
今年は、とても忙しかったよ
This year was really busy for me.

そうだよね
Yeah, I could tell.

まいにちおそ　　　　　　しごとたいへん
毎日遅くまで仕事大変そうだったもんね
Your job seemed tough, with late nights and all.

らいねん　　　　すこ
来年はもう少しゆっくりしたい
I want to take it a bit slower next year.

ハハ、そうだね
Haha, yeah, right.

らいねん　もくひょう
ネコちゃん来年の目標はあるの?
Neko-chan, do you have any goals for next year?

き
まだ決めてないけど・・・
I haven't decided yet,

まいにち
毎日ヨガをすることかな・・・
but maybe... do yoga every day?

それいいね!
That's a great idea!

つぎあ　　　　　としあ
次会うのは年明けだね!
Our next meeting will be in the new year!

とし
じゃあ、よいお年を
Well then, have a great New Year.

とし
よいお年を!
You too, have a great New Year

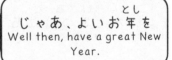

61

ネコちゃんは家<ruby>家<rt>いえ</rt></ruby>の<ruby>前<rt>まえ</rt></ruby>にいますよ
Neko-chan is in front of the house.

ここから<ruby>少<rt>すこ</rt></ruby>し<ruby>遠<rt>とお</rt></ruby>いです
It's a little far from here.

シカちゃんは<ruby>木<rt>き</rt></ruby>の<ruby>後<rt>うし</rt></ruby>ろにいますよ
Shika-chan is behind the tree.

スーパーは<ruby>近<rt>ちか</rt></ruby>くにありますよ
Supermarket is nearby.

リモコンはテレビの<ruby>横<rt>よこ</rt></ruby>にありますよ
The remote control is next to the TV.

この<ruby>辺<rt>あた</rt></ruby>りにコンビニはありますか？
Is there a convenience store around here?

シバくんはシカちゃんの<ruby>隣<rt>となり</rt></ruby>にいますよ
Shiba-kun is next to Shika-chan.

<ruby>鍵<rt>かぎ</rt></ruby>はここにありますよ
The key is here.

<ruby>向<rt>む</rt></ruby>かいのビルの<ruby>前<rt>まえ</rt></ruby>で<ruby>待<rt>ま</rt></ruby>っていてください
Please wait in front of the building across the street.

そこに<ruby>忘<rt>わす</rt></ruby>れ<ruby>物<rt>もの</rt></ruby>がありますよ
There is something forgotten there.

<ruby>消<rt>け</rt></ruby>しゴムは<ruby>本<rt>ほん</rt></ruby>と<ruby>本<rt>ほん</rt></ruby>の<ruby>間<rt>あいだ</rt></ruby>にありました
The eraser was between the books.

あそこにねこちゃんがいますよ
Neko-chan is over there.

シバくんは<ruby>家<rt>いえ</rt></ruby>の<ruby>外<rt>そと</rt></ruby>にいますよ
Shiba-kun is outside the house.

<ruby>入口<rt>いりぐち</rt></ruby>はあちらです
Entrance is that way.

シバくんは<ruby>家<rt>いえ</rt></ruby>の<ruby>中<rt>なか</rt></ruby>にいました
Shiba-kun was inside the house.

<ruby>出口<rt>でぐち</rt></ruby>はこちらです
The exit is this way.

道路を渡りましょう
Let's cross the street.

バス停でバスを待っています
I'm waiting for the bus at the bus stop.

信号が赤ですので止まってください
The traffic light is red, so please stop.

信号が青になりましたよ
The traffic light turned green.

この道は一方通行ですよ
This road is one way.

近くに駐車場はありますか?
Is there a parking lot nearby?

歩道を歩いてください
Please walk on the sidewalk.

この先は行き止まりです
This way is a dead end.

大阪は日本の西側にあります
Osaka is located on the western side of Japan.

東京は日本の東側にあります
Tokyo is located on the eastern side of Japan.

次の道を左に曲がってください
Turn left at the next street.

次の橋を右に曲がってください
Turn right at the next bridge.

公園で子供達が遊んでいます
Children are playing in the park.

自動販売機でお茶を買います
I buy green tea from the vending machine.

タクシー乗り場はどこですか?
Where is the taxi stand?

この住所までお願いします
To this address please.

いらっしゃいませ
Welcome

給油できました
The refueling is complete.

ありがとうございます
Thank you.

レギュラー満たんでお願いします
Fill it up with regular gasoline, please.

5300円です
That'll be 5300 yen

はい
Sure.

ありがとうございます
Thank you.

給油口を開けてください
Please open the fuel lid.

どちら方面に行かれますか?
Which direction are you headed?

フロントガラスをお拭きしましょうか?
Would you like me to clean the windshield?

名古屋方面で
Direction to Nagoya.

はい、お願いします
Yes, please.

では、こちらの方へ
Then this way please.

ゴミはありますか?
Do you have any trash?

ありがとうございました
Thank you very much.

はい、あります
Yes, I do

64

えいご　はな
英語を話せますか？
Do you speak English?

じしん
地震です
It's an earthquake

けいさつ　よ
警察を呼んでください
Please call the police.

かじ
火事です
There's fire

たす
助けてください
Please help me.

つなみ
津波がきています
There's a tsunami coming.

きゅうきゅうしゃ　よ
救急車を呼んでください
Call an ambulance, please.

ひなん
避難してください
Please evacuate.

さいふ
財布をなくしました
I lost my wallet.

かぞく　　ゆくえふめい
家族が行方不明です
My family is missing.

にもつ　わす
タクシーに荷物を忘れました
I left my luggage in the taxi.

あんぜん　ばしょ　いどう
安全な場所に移動してください
Please move to a safe location.

けいさつ
警察はどこですか？
Where is the police station?

しょうぼうしゃ　よ
消防車を呼んでください
Please call the fire department.

けいたいでんわ　ぬす
携帯電話を盗まれました
My cell phone was stolen.

けがにん
怪我人がいます
There are injured people.

65

あしたたの
明日楽しみだね!
I'm excited about tomorrow!

うん、今行くね
Great, I'm coming out now.

うん
Yeah.

ブルくんに会えて嬉しい!
I'm so glad to see you, Bull-kun!

何時に待ち合わせする?
What time should we meet up?

うん
Yeah,

十時でいい?
Is 10 o'clock okay?

僕もタヌキちゃんに会えて嬉しい
I'm also happy to see you, Tanuki-chan.

うん、いいよ
Yeah, that works.

じゃあ行こっか
Shall we go?

じゃあ十時に家に迎えに行くね
I'll pick you up at your house at 10 then.

海、久しぶりに行くよ
I haven't been to the beach in a while.

うん、ありがとう!
Sure, thanks!

今日お弁当作ってきたんだ
I brought homemade bento today.

着いたよー!
I've arrived!

ヤッター
Yay!

66

ありがとう
Thank you.

作ってくれてありがとう
Thanks for making it.

じゃあ着いたら海辺で食べよう
Let's have it by the beach when we arrive.

夜はレストランを予約してるから
We have a reservation at a restaurant for dinner tonight.

着いたよー
We've arrived.

うん!楽しみ
Yeah! I can't wait.

わー綺麗ー!
Wow, it's beautiful!

わー幸せだなぁ
Wow, I feel so happy.

海の音と潮風が気持ちいい
The sound of the waves and the sea breeze feel so good.

うん!幸せだね
Yeah, I do too.

そうだね
Indeed.

この時間がずっと続くといいのに
I wish this moment could last forever.

あの辺に座る?
How about sitting over there?

そうだね
You are right.

うん
Sure.

お弁当食べよー
Let's eat the bento.

あっという間に夜だね
Nighttime came so quickly.

うん
Yeah.

夜の海もすごくいいね
The night sea is also very nice.

うわー美味しそう
Wow, it looks delicious.

うん
Yeah.

67

LOVE

ネコちゃんのことが好きです
I like you Neko-chan.

ネコちゃんのことが大好きです
I like you very much Neko-chan.

ネコちゃんを愛しています
I love you Neko-chan.

ネコちゃんに恋をしています
I'm in love with Neko-chan.

ネコちゃんに一目ぼれしました
I fell in love at first sight with Neko-chan.

明日ネコちゃんに告白しようと思うんだ
I'm planning to ask Neko-chan out tomorrow.

シバくんに告白されたんだ
Shiba-kun asked me out.

ネコちゃんのことがずっと好きでした
I've always loved you Neko-chan.

付き合ってもらえませんか?
Will you go out with me?

私と付き合ってください
Will you go out with me?

デートしませんか?
Do you want to go on a date?

ずっと一緒にいたいよ
I want to be with you forever.

ネコちゃんのことが全部好きです
I love everything about you Neko-chan.

シバくん カッコいいね
Shiba-kun, you are cool.

結婚してください
Will you marry me?

ネコちゃん綺麗だね
Neko-chan, you look beautiful.

68

Heartbreak

かれし わか
彼氏と別れました
I broke up with my boyfriend.

かのじょ わか
彼女と別れたばかりなんだ
I've just broken up with my girlfriend.

かのじょ わか
彼女と別れました
I broke up with my girlfriend.

きみ じんせい かんが
君がいない人生なんて考えられない
I can't imagine a life without you.

あ
もう会えません
I can't see you anymore.

いちどかんが なお
もう一度考え直して
Please reconsider one more time.

りこん
離婚しました
I've divorced.

まだネコちゃんのことが好きです
I still love about you Neko-chan.

わか
もう別れよ
I want to break up.

た なお
もう立ち直れない
I can't recover from this anymore.

しつれん
失恋しました
I've had a heartbreak.

わたし かれし
私には彼氏がいます
I have a boyfriend.

きのう ふ
昨日、ネコちゃんに振られたんだ
Yesterday, Neko-chan dumped me.

わたし かのじょ
私には彼女がいます
I have a girlfriend.

わたし わか
私と別れてほしい
I want you to break up with me.

わたし つ あ ひと
私には付き合ってる人がいます
I'm seeing someone.

69

すごく嬉しいです
I'm so happy.

素晴らしい
Awesome. / Wonderful.

楽しみです
I can't wait. / I'm looking forward to it.

完璧です
Perfect.

ワクワクします
I'm excited.

感動しました
I was impressed.

ドキドキします
I'm nervous, excited.

泣けました
It made me cry.

落ち込んでいます
I'm feeling down.

驚きました
I'm amazed. / I'm surprised.

すごく悲しいです
I'm really sad.

びっくりしました
I'm surprised.

がっかりしました
I was disappointed.

羨ましいです
I'm jealous.

寂しいです
I feel lonely.

退屈です
I'm bored.

Feelings
Casual

すごく嬉しい
I'm so happy.

楽しみ
I can't wait. / I'm looking forward to it.

ワクワクする
I'm excited.

ドキドキする
I'm nervous, excited.

落ち込んでるんだ
I'm feeling down.

すごく悲しい
I'm really sad.

がっかりした
I was disappointed.

寂しいよ
I feel lonely.

腹が立つ
I'm angry.

すごい
Awesome. / Amazing.

完璧だね
Perfect.

感動したよ
I was impressed.

泣けちゃった
It made me cry.

驚いたよ
I'm amazed. / I'm surprised.

びっくりした
I'm surprised.

羨ましい
I'm jealous.

めんどくさい
I can't be bothered. / What a pain.

退屈だ
I'm bored.

いらっしゃいませ
Welcome.

<ruby>何<rt>なん</rt></ruby><ruby>名<rt>めい</rt></ruby><ruby>様<rt>さま</rt></ruby>ですか？
How many people?

<ruby>二人<rt>ふたり</rt></ruby>です
Table for two, please.

こちらにお<ruby>名前<rt>なまえ</rt></ruby>を<ruby>書<rt>か</rt></ruby>いてください
Please write your name here.

あちらでお<ruby>待<rt>ま</rt></ruby>ちください
Please wait over there.

シバ<ruby>様<rt>さま</rt></ruby>、お<ruby>席<rt>せき</rt></ruby>がご<ruby>用意<rt>ようい</rt></ruby>できました
Shiba-sama, your table is ready.

はい
Yes.

こちらの<ruby>席<rt>せき</rt></ruby>へどうぞ
Please follow me to your table.

こちらがメニューです
Here's the menu.

ご<ruby>注文<rt>ちゅうもん</rt></ruby>がお<ruby>決<rt>き</rt></ruby>まりになりましたら、
When you're ready to order,

そちらのボタンでお<ruby>呼<rt>よ</rt></ruby>びください
Please press the button over there to call us.

ご<ruby>注文<rt>ちゅうもん</rt></ruby>を<ruby>伺<rt>うかが</rt></ruby>いいたします
May I take your order?

<ruby>私<rt>わたし</rt></ruby>はオムライスをお<ruby>願<rt>ねが</rt></ruby>いします
I'll take omelette with rice, please.

<ruby>僕<rt>ぼく</rt></ruby>はカレーをお<ruby>願<rt>ねが</rt></ruby>いします
I'll take curry, please.

72

カレーの辛（から）さを1から10まででお選（えら）びいただけます
You can choose the spiciness of the curry from 1 to 10.

10でお願（ねが）いします
I'll take level ten please.

ごゆっくりどうぞ
Please take your time.
(Enjoy your meal.)

カレーどう?
How's the curry?

お飲（の）み物（もの）はいかがされますか?
Would you like anything to drink?

ウーロン茶（ちゃ）二（ふた）つお願（ねが）いします
Two oolong teas, please.

辛（から）いけど美味（おい）しいよ
It's really spicy but it's good.

かしこまりました
Certainly.

烏龍茶（ウーロンちゃ）です
Oolong teas.

めっちゃ汗（あせ）かいてるじゃん
You are sweating a lot!

はい
Yes.

カレーです
Here's your curry.

めっちゃ辛（から）い笑
It's super spicy haha.

ハハハハ
Hahaha.

はい
Yes.

オムライスです
Omelette with rice.

クリームソーダをください
Can I have a cream soda, please?

73

あした ふたり よやく ねが
明日、二人で予約をお願いします
I'd like to make a reservation for two tomorrow.

みず
お水をください
Water please.

じかん
お時間はいかがなさいますか？
What time?

ちゅうもん き
ご注文はお決まりですか？
May I take your order?

しちじ ねが
七時にお願いします
At seven please.

おい
美味しそう
It looks delicious.

なまえ うかが
お名前を伺えますか？
May I have your name?

わたし
私は〜アレルギーです
I'm allergic to 〜.

らいてん ま
ご来店お待ちしております
We look forward to seeing you at the store.

お
ナイフを落としてしまいました
I dropped the knife.

まんせき
ただいま満席です
We are currently full.

これをもらえますか？
Can I have this one?

えいご
英語のメニューはありますか？
Do you have an English menu?

どのワインがおすすめですか？
Which wine would you recommend?

りょうり なん
おすすめの料理は何ですか？
What dishes do you recommend?

さら さ
お皿を下げてもよろしいですか？
May I take your plate?

おい
美味しいです
It's delicious.

おい
美味しかったです
It was delicious.

おい　　　　　　まず
美味しくない / 不味い
It's not so good.

なか
お腹がすきました
I'm hungry.

から
このカレーは辛いです
This curry is spicy.

なか
お腹がいっぱいです
I'm full.

あま
このケーキは甘いです
This cake is sweet.

のど　かわ
喉が渇きました
I'm thirsty.

しょ
このスープは塩っぱいです
This soup is salty.

にく　やわ
この肉は柔らかいです
This meat is tender.

あぶら
このラーメンは油っこいです
This ramen is oily.

にく
この肉はかたいです
This meat is hard.

にが
このコーヒーは苦いです
This coffee is bitter.

あつ
このスープは熱いです
This soup is hot.

うめぼ　　す
梅干しは酸っぱいです
These pickled plums are sour.

ちゃ つめ
このお茶は冷たいです
This green tea is cold.

いらっしゃいませ
Welcome.

サラダかポテトをお選びいただけます
You can choose between salad or fries.

店内でお召し上がりですか？
For here?

ポテトをお願いします
I'll go with fries, please.

持ち帰りです
To go.

お飲み物と
for the drink and,

ポテトのサイズはいかがされますか？
for the fries, what size would you like?

ご注文をお伺いいたします
May I take your order?

どっちもMサイズでお願いします
Both in medium, please.

チーズバーガーのセットをお願いします
I'll have the Cheeseburger combo, please.

飲み物はコーラを下さい
For the drink, I'd like a Cola, please.

以上でよろしいでしょうか？
Is that all?

76

はい
Yes.

かしこまりました
Got it.

すみません
Excuse me.

お会計は５８０円です
Your total is 580 yen.

コーラを頼んだんですが
I ordered a cola but,

６００円お預かりします
Here's 600 yen.

オレンジジュースが入っていました
There was orange juice in it.

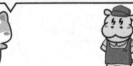

２０円のお釣りとレシートです
Here's your change of 20yen and the receipt.

こちらの番号札でお待ちください
Please wait with this number card.

申し訳ございません
I'm so sorry.

すぐにコーラをお持ちします
I'll get you a cola right away.

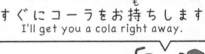

番号札三番のお客様
number 3 on the number card.

チーズバーガーのセットです
Here's your Cheeseburger combo.

ありがとうございます
Thank you.

ありがとうございます
Thank you.

いらっしゃいませ
Welcome.

ご注文をお伺いいたします
ちゅうもん　うかが
May I take your order?

アイスコーヒーをお願いします
ねが
I'd like an iced coffee, please.

サイズはいかがなさいますか?
What size would you like?

Ｌサイズ、お願いします
える　　　ねが
Large size, please.

かしこまりました
Got it.

あとスコーンもお願いします
ねが
Also, I'd like a scone, please.

以上でよろしいでしょうか?
いじょう
Alright, will that be all?

はい
Yes.

スコーンは温めますか?
あたた
Would you like the scone to be warmed?

78

はい、お願いします
Yes, please.

お会計は780円です
Your total is 780 yen.

カードで支払います
I'll pay with a credit card.

◀ Credit card

砂糖とミルクをもらえますか？
Can I have some sugar and milk, please?

暗証番号をお願いします
Could you please enter your PIN?

あちらのカウンターでご用意しております
We have them available at the counter over there.

はい
Yes.

ご自由にお取りください
Please feel free to help yourself.

ありがとうございます
Thank you.

わかりました
Got it.

あちらでお待ちください
Please wait over there.

ストローもそこにありますか？
Are straws available there as well?

アイスコーヒーとスコーンです
Here is your iced coffee and scone.

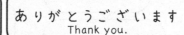

はい、ございます
Yes, we do have straws there too.

ありがとうございます
Thank you.

お疲れー
To your hard work.

つまみは？
And for appetisers?

お疲れ様です
To your hard work too.

そうですねー
Hmm.

今日も大変だったねー
It was tough day today, huh?

枝豆とか？
How about edamame?

そうですね
Yes, It was.

じゃあ、枝豆も
Okay, edamame too, please.

何飲む？
What do you want to drink?

はい
Sure.

ビールで
Beer, please.

お待たせしました
Thank you for waiting.

すみませーん
Excuse me.

ビール二つと枝豆です
Here are two draft beers and edamame.

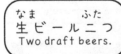
生ビール二つ
Two draft beers.

80

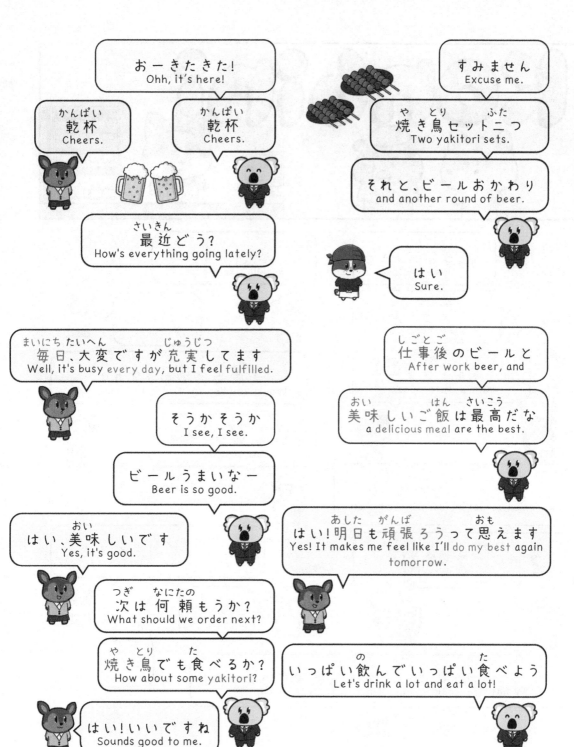

いらっしゃいませ
Welcome.

べんとういってん
お弁当一点
One bento.

ポテトチップス一点
One potato chips.

あと、アイスカフェラテと
And Can I also get an iced cafe latte and

からあ　ひと
唐揚げ一つください
One karaage (fried chicken) please.

アイスカフェラテのサイズはいかがなさいますか？
What size would you like for the iced cafe latte?

えむ
Mサイズで
Medium size please.

はい
Alright.

べんとう　あたた
お弁当は温めますか？
Would you like the bento to be heated?

ねが
はい、お願いします
Yes, please.

ぶくろ　　　　りょう
レジ袋はご利用ですか？
Would you like a plastic bag?

はい
Yes.

お会計1080円です
The total is 1,080yen.

じゃあ僕はこれお願いします
Alright, then I'll have this.

そちらにお金をいれてください
Please put the money there.

よろしければOKボタンを押してください
If it's alright with you, please press the OK button.

ビール二点、ミックスナッツ一点
Two beers, one pack of mixed nuts.

はい
Yes.

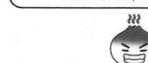

肉まんも一つください
and also one meat bun, please.

ありがとうございました
Thank you very much.

お会計1200円です
The total is 1,200yen.

カッパくんもう買ったの?
Did you already buy Kappa-kun?

年齢確認ボタンを押してください
Please press the age verification button.

はい
Yes.

うん
Yeah.

ありがとうございました
Thank you very much.

すみません
Excuse me.

はい
Yes.

こうざ　かいせつ
口座を開設したいのですが
I want to open an account.

も
パスポートを持ってきました
I brought my passport.

はい、かしこまりました
Yes, certainly.

ようし　　　　　きにゅう　ねが
こちらの用紙にご記入お願いいたします
Please fill out this form here.

ありがとうございます
Thank you very much.

はい
Sure.

かくにん
確認いたします
Let me check.

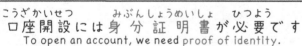

こうざかいせつ　　　　　みぶんしょうめいしょ　ひつよう
口座開設には身分証明書が必要です
To open an account, we need proof of identity.

うんてんめんきょしょう
運転免許証またはパスポートをお持ちですか？
Do you have a driver's license or passport?

も

では、こちらの書類を確認の上、
So, please review these documents,

こちらに印鑑をお願いします
Please name stamp here.

では、手続きは後ほどいたします
We'll proceed with the process later.

すみません
I'm sorry.

次回ご来店時、こちらの紙をお持ちください
Please bring this paper with you on your next visit.

印鑑を持っていません
I don't have a name stamp.

わかりました
Understood.

ご来店、ありがとうございました
Thank you for coming in.

そうですか
I see.

A few days later

口座開設されるには印鑑が必要です
You'll need a name stamp for the account opening.

すみません
Excuse me

わかりました
Understood.

印鑑を持ってきました
I brought a name stamp.

後日、印鑑を作って持ってきます
I'll make a name stamp and come back later.

しば

かしこまりました
Certainly.

ありがとうございます
Thank you.

こちらに印鑑を押してください
Please stamp here.

お待たせ
Sorry for the wait!

えっと、カメラは何階にあるんだろー
Hmm, I wonder which floor the cameras are on.

元気？
How are you?

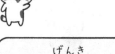

あそこにフロアマップあるよ
There's a floor map over there.

うん、元気だよー
Yeah! I'm good, thanks!

三階だって
It says it's on the third floor.

今日は来てくれてありがとう！
Thanks for coming today!

エスカレーターで三階まで行こっ
Let's take the escalator up to the third floor!

全然いいよー！
No problem at all!

あっ！カメラあったよ
Oh, I see some cameras here.

店はあっちだよー
The store is over there.

行こっかー
Shall we go?

いっぱいあるねー
There are so many!

このカメラどう思う?
What do you think of this camera?

これ、何か知ってる?
Do you know what is this?

かっこいい
It looks cool.

ヘッドマッサージするやつだよ
It's a head massager.

この中でどれがいいと思う?
Which one do you think is good among these?

そうなんだ
I see

機能性はどれもあまり変わらないんだ
The functionality doesn't vary much among them.

気持ちいいのかなぁ
I wonder if it feels good.

見た目ではこれが一番いいと思う
By looks, I think this one is the best.

けっこう持ってる人多いよ
Lots of people have it

じゃあこれにするよ
Okay, I'll go with this one.

そうなんだ
Interesting.

うん
Yeah.

じゃあ、誕生日楽しみにしてるね
Well, I'm looking forward to my birthday then.

何か他にもみて行く?
Do you want to check out anything else?

えっ! それどういうこと?
Eh! what do you mean by that?

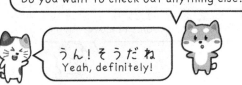

うん!そうだね
Yeah, definitely!

ハハハ
Hahaha

いらっしゃいませ
Welcome.

しょうしょう ま
はい、少々お待ちください
Yes, please wait a moment.

なに さが
何かお探しでしょうか？
Are you looking for something?

ざいこ かくにん
在庫を確認いたします
Let me check the stock.

ありがとうございます
Thank you.

ティー くつ さが
Ｔシャツと靴を探しています
I'm looking for a T-shirt and shoes.

エム
Ｍサイズ、ございます
Yes, we have it in size Medium.

ティー たな
Ｔシャツはこちらの棚にございます
T-shirts are on this shelf over here.

くつ
靴はこちらです
The shoes are right here.

しちゃく
試着してもいいですか？
Can I try it on?

ありがとうございます
Thank you

ティー エム
このＴシャツのＭサイズはありますか？
Do you have this T-shirt in size M?

しちゃくしつ
試着室はあちらです
The fitting rooms are over there.

ありがとうございます
Thank you.

サイズピッタリでした
It fits perfectly.

よかったです
I'm glad to hear that.

あのスニーカーの24cmありますか？
セ ン チ
Do you have that sneakers in size 24 cm?

はい、確認いたします
か く に ん
Let me check for you.

在庫がございますのでお持ちいたします
ざ い こ　　　　　　　　　　　　　　　　も
Yes, we have it in stock, I'll bring it to you.

ありがとうございます
Thank you

靴をお持ちしました
く つ　　も
I have brought the shoes.

ちょっと大きいです
お お
It's a bit big.

もう少し小さいサイズはありますか？
す こ　ち い
Do you have a slightly smaller size?

はい、確認いたします
か く に ん
Sure, let me check.

こちら23.5cmです
セ ン チ
Here's a pair in size 23.5 cm.

ありがとうございます
Thank you.

サイズ、ちょうどいいです
This size is just right.

このTシャツと靴をください
ティー　　　　　　く つ
I'll take this T-shirt and the shoes.

ありがとうございます
Thank you.

ポイントカードはお持ちでしょうか？
も
Do you have our point card?

いいえ
No, I don't.

お作りになられますか？
つ く
Would you like to make one?

また今度で
こ ん ど
Maybe next time.

89

Fashion

<table>
<tr>
<td>

何を着るか決められないです
I can't decide what to wear.

</td>
<td>

同じ鞄を二つ持っています
I have two identical bags.

</td>
</tr>
<tr>
<td>

汗をいっぱいかいたので服を脱ぎました
I sweated a lot, so I took off my clothes.

</td>
<td>

眼鏡はどこですか？
Where are my glasses?

</td>
</tr>
<tr>
<td>

私の学校の制服は地味です
My school uniform is plain.

</td>
<td>

玄関で靴を履きました
I put on my shoes at the entrance.

</td>
</tr>
<tr>
<td>

日差しが強いので、帽子を被ってください
The sun is strong, so please wear a hat.

</td>
<td>

試着してもいいですか？
May I try the clothes on?

</td>
</tr>
<tr>
<td>

これはちょうどいいサイズです
This is a perfect size.

</td>
<td>

ただいま、品切れ中です
We are currently out of stock.

</td>
</tr>
<tr>
<td>

シバくんは派手な服が好きです
Shiba-kun likes flashy clothes.

</td>
<td>

ネックレスをつけたいですか？
Do you want to wear a necklace?

</td>
</tr>
<tr>
<td>

雨が降っているので、傘をさします
It's raining, so I'll use an umbrella.

</td>
<td>

セーターを探しています
I'm looking for a sweater.

</td>
</tr>
<tr>
<td>

靴下を左右間違えて履いていました
I was wearing socks on the opposite feet.

</td>
<td>

よくお似合いです
It looks great on you.

</td>
</tr>
</table>

どっちがいいと思いますか？
Which one do you think is better?

予算オーバーです
It's over my budget.

見ているだけです
I'm just looking.

これはどうですか？
What about this one?

少し考えます
I'll think about it.

このSサイズはありますか？
Do you have this one for size small?

この素材は何ですか？
What is this material?

試着室はどこですか？
Where is the fitting room?

いかがですか？
How do you like it?

袖が少し長いです
The sleeves are little long.

ズボンの丈が短いです
The pants are too short.

もっと小さいサイズはありますか？
Do you have a smaller size?

他の色はありますか？
Do you have any other Colors?

この商品はセール対象品ですか？
Is this item on sale?

少し大きいです
It's a little big.

ウエストがきついです
The waist is tight.

91

こんにちは
Hello.

きにゅう　　ねが
こちらにご記入をお願いいたします
Please fill out this form.

さんじ　　　　よやく
三時から予約してますライオンです
I have an appointment at 3 o'clock,
it's under the name Lion.

はい
Yes.

か
書きました
I've written it.

ライオン様お待ちしておりました
Lion-sama, we've been waiting for you.

ありがとうございます
Thank you very much.

らいてん
ご来店ありがとうございます
Thank you for coming to our hair salon.

しょうしょう　ま
こちらで少々お待ちください
Please wait here for a moment.

とうてん　　　りよう　はじ
当店のご利用は初めてでしょうか?
Is this your first time here?

さま　　　せき
ライオン様こちらのお席へどうぞ
Lion-sama, please follow me to your seat.

はい
Yes.

ほんじつ
本日はいかがいたしましょうか?
What can I do for you today?

カットとカラーをお願（ねが）いします
I'd like a haircut and coloring.

わかりました
Alright.

では先（さき）にシャンプーします
Let's start with a shampoo first.

どれくらい切（き）りましょうか？
How much should I cut?

こちらへどうぞ
Please come this way.

この写真（しゃしん）の人（ひと）くらいまで切（き）ってください
Please cut it to be about as short as the person in this picture.

はい
Okay.

次（つぎ）にカラーをします
Next, I'll do coloring.

おっ！かっこいいですね
Oh! That looks cool.

はい
Okay.

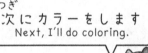

わかりました
Understood.

カラーはどうしますか？
What about the coloring?

どうでしょうか？
How do you like it?

完璧（かんぺき）です！
It's perfect!

カラーもこの写真（しゃしん）の人（ひと）みたいに
I'd like the coloring to be like the person in this picture too.

ありがとうございます
Thank you.

Hair

きょう かみ そ
今日、髪を染めました
I dyed my hair today.

かゆ
痒いところはございませんか?
Is it itchy anywhere?

かみ の
髪を伸ばしたいです
I want to grow my hair longer.

かみがた
どんな髪型がおすすめですか?
What kind of hairstyle would you recommend?

かみ き
そろそろ、髪を切りたいです
I need to get a haircut soon.

かみいろ あか
髪色を明るくしてください
Please make the hair color lighter.

センチ き
〜cm切ってください
Please cut 〜cm.

かみいろ くら
髪色を暗くしてください
Please make the hair color darker.

パーマをあてました
I got a perm.

みじか
もっと短くしてください
Please cut it shorter.

しらが そ
白髪を染めてください
Please dye my gray hairs.

マッサージをしてもいいですか?
Can I give you a massage?

まえがみ の
前髪は伸ばしています
I'm growing out my bangs.

ざい
スタイリング剤をつけていいですか?
Can I use styling products?

けさき いた
毛先が傷んでいます
The ends of my hair are damaged.

かみがた にあ おも
この髪型は似合うと思いますか?
Do you think this hairstyle suits me?

94

Hair

髪型変えたいんだよねー
I want to change my hairstyle.

それか、前髪を短くしようかな
or maybe I'll cut my bangs short.

どんな髪型にしたいの？
What kind of hairstyle are you thinking of?

前髪あるの見たことない
I've never seen you with bangs.

そうなの
That's right.

まだ決めてないんだけど・・・
I haven't decided yet...

やったことないの
I've never tried it.

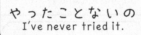

迷ってるんだ
You're still undecided.

やってみたら？
How about giving it a try?

うん
Yeah.

かなりイメチェンになるんじゃない？
It could be a significant makeover.

今長いから、短くしてもいいかなって
My hair is long right now, so maybe I could go shorter.

じゃあそうしてみる
Alright, I'll give it a shot.

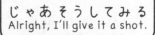

いいんじゃない？
I think it's good idea

いらっしゃいませ
Welcome

_{なに} _{さが}
何かお探しですか？
Are you looking for something?

そうですか
I see.

_{ため}
試してみます
I'll give it a try.

これ、ください
I'll take this one.

ファンデーションとチークを探^{さが}しています
I'm looking for foundation and blush.

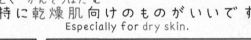

_{とく} _{かんそうはだ} _む
特に乾燥肌向けのものがいいです
Especially for dry skin.

ありがとうございます
Thank you very much.

_{いろみ}
お色味はこちらでよろしいですか
Is this color okay for you?

こちらのファンデーションはいかがですか？
How about this foundation?

_{かんそうはだ} _{かた} _{にんき} _{しょうひん}
乾燥肌の方に人気な商品です
It's quite popular among those with dry skin.

_{だいじょうぶ}
はい、大丈夫です
Yes, that's fine.

96

同じブランドのチークです
It's the same brand of blush.

他店に在庫がございます
Good news! Another store has it in stock,

このような色がございます
It comes in these colors.

一週間でご用意できます
and we can have it ready for you in a week.

この色いいですね
This color looks nice.

申し訳ございませんが
I'm sorry but

はい、お願いします
Great, please do that.

こちらの色は、只今品切れしております
This color is currently out of stock.

そうなんですね
Oh, I see.

お取り置きしておきます
We'll keep it aside for you.

それは残念です
That's too bad.

こちらに氏名、電話番号、住所をご記入ください
Could you please write
your name, phone number, and address here?

他店に在庫があるか確認いたしましょうか？
Would you like me to check if other stores have it in stock?

では、来週
Then next week.

またのご来店おまちしております
We look forward to seeing you again.

はい、お願いします
Yes, please

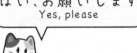

はい、ありがとうございます
Yes, thank you.

すみません
Excuse me

はい
Yes?

それなら、こちらの風邪薬がおすすめです
In that case, I recommend this cold medicine.

ありがとうございます
Thank you.

あのー風邪薬を探してるんですが
Um, I'm looking for cold medicine.

ご使用方法はしっかり読んでくださいね
Please make sure to read the instructions carefully.

どのような症状がありますか?
Sure. What kind of symptoms do you have?

あと痛み止めも欲しいです
Also, I'd like to get some pain killers.

喉が痛くて、鼻水もでてます
I have a sore throat and runny nose.

痛み止めはこちらです
Pain killers are over here.

お大事になさってください
Take care of yourself.

98

いたたたー
Ouch...

ある
歩ける?
Can you walk?

どうしたの?
What happened?

だいじょうぶ
大丈夫?
Are you okay?

ある
うん、歩けるよ
Yeah, I can walk.

うん
Yeah

いちばんちか　やっきょくしら
一番近くの薬局調べるね
Let me find the nearest pharmacy.

さっき、あそこでつまずいちゃって
Earlier, I tripped over there.

ちか
あっ!近くにある
Oh! There's one nearby.

けが
あー怪我してる
Oh! You are hurting.

ばんそうこう　しょうどくえき
えっと、絆創膏と消毒液がいる
Let's see, I need band-aid and disinfection.

やっきょく い
薬局に行こう
Let's go to the pharmacy.

か
買ってきたよ!
I got them!

ありがとう
Thanks.

うん
Yeah.

たす
助かったよ
I appreciate your help.

99

こんにちは
Hello.

こんにちは
Hello.

問診票にご記入をお願いします
Please fill out this medical questionnaire.

きょう
今日はどうなさいましたか？
How can I help you today?

きにゅう お も
記入を終えたらお持ちください
Please bring it to us when you are done.

なまえ よ
お名前が呼ばれるまで
Until we call your name,

かぜ ながび
風邪が長引いてて
I have a lingering cold.

せき か ま
あちらの席でお掛けになってお待ちください
Please have a seat over there and wait.

わかりました
I see.

はい
Yes.

りょう はじ
こちらのクリニックのご利用は初めてですか？
Is this your first time visit to this clinic?

はい
Yes.

ネズミさん
Nezumi-san.

ほけんしょう も
保険証はお持ちですか？
Do you have your health insurance card?

しんさつしつ まえ ま
診察室の前でお待ちください
please wait in front of the examination room.

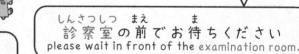

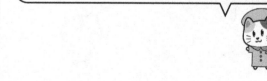

ネズミさんお入りください
Nezumi-san, please come in.

はい
Yes.

今日はどうなさいましたか？
How can I help you today?

風邪が長引いてて
I have a lingering cold.

どのような症状がありますか？
Sure. What kind of symptoms do you have?

お腹が痛いのと
I've been having stomach ache and...

鼻水とくしゃみが止まりません
I can't stop sniffing and sneezing.

体温ははかりましたか？
Have you taken your temperature?

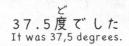

37.5度でした
It was 37,5 degrees.

熱は高くないですね
Ok, the fever is not high.

口を開けてください
Open your mouth.

少し腫れてますね
A little swollen.

薬を出しますね
I'll give you some medicine.

食後に一錠ずつ飲んでください
Take one pill after each meal.

先生ありがとうございます
Thank you very much, doctor.

お大事になさってください
Take care of yourself.

はい
Yes.

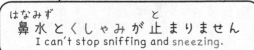

101

ここに座ってください
Please sit down here.

気分はどうですか？
How do you feel?

ここに寝てください
Please lie back here.

どんな症状ですか？
What is the symptoms?

後ろを向いてください
Please turn around.

採血をします
I'll take your blood sample.

アレルギーはありますか？
Do you have any allergies?

熱を測ります
I will take your temperature.

薬は薬局でもらってください
Please get the medicine at the pharmacy.

今飲んでいる薬はありますか？
Are you currently taking any medication?

処方箋を出しますね
I will write a prescription for you.

ここを動かすと痛いですか？
Does it hurt when I move here?

注射を打ちます
I'll give you an injection.

ここを押すと痛いですか？
Does it hurt when I press here?

手術が必要です
You need an operation.

血が出ています
You're bleeding.

102

こんにちは、シバさん
Hello, Shiba-san

検査を詳しく行ったほうがいいですね
It might be better to conduct more detailed tests.

たいちょう
体調はどうですか？
How are you feeling?

いま じょうたい
今の状態からいくと
Based on your current condition,

あまりよくないです
Not well.

にゅういん すす
入院をお勧めします
I recommend hospitalization.

きかん
どのくらいの期間ですか？
How long will it be?

しょうじょう
どんな症状がでていますか？
What symptoms do you have?

よそく むずか
予測が難しいですが、
It's hard to predict,

さいてい いっしゅうかん とおか
最低でも一週間から十日ほど
but a hospitalization of at least one week to ten days may be.

むね いた いきぎ つづ
胸の痛みと、息切れが続いています
I've been having chest pain and shortness of breath.

けんさ けっかしだい きかん か
検査の結果次第で期間が変わることもあります
The duration may change depending on the test results.

そうですか
I see.

わ
分かりました
I understood.

Sick

きぶん
気分がよくありません
I'm not feeling well.

きゅうきゅうしゃ　よ
救急車を呼んでください
Call an ambulance, please.

ねつ
熱があります
I have a fever.

くしゃみが出ています
I'm sneezing.

かぜ
風邪をひきました
I have a cold.

くすり　の　　　　くだ
薬を飲んで下さい
Please take your medicine.

やけど
火傷をしました
I got burned.

なか　いた
お腹が痛いです
I have a stomach ache.

さむけ
寒気がします
I feel cold.

はなみず　で
鼻水が出ます
I have a runny nose.

めまいがします
I feel dizzy.

あたま　いた
頭が痛いです
I have a headache.

せき　で
咳が出てます
I have a cough.

は　け
吐き気がします
I feel nauseous.

いた
ここが痛いです
It's painful here.

なお
どれくらいで治りますか?
How long will it take to get better?

104

どうしたの?
What's wrong?

今日は早めに帰ったほうがいいよ
Maybe you should go home early today.

具合悪いの?
Are you feeling unwell?

うん、ごめんね
Yeah, sorry about that.

うん、風邪ひいちゃった
Yeah, I caught a cold.

謝らなくていいよ
No need to apologize.

早く用事だけ済ませよう
Let's finish our tasks quickly.

あらー、季節の変わり目だもんね
Oh, it's the change of seasons right?

One hour later

そう、温度差が激しいから
That's right. The temperature difference is quite extreme.

後は、一人でできるから
The rest, I can handle myself

帰って休んで!
So go home and rest!

朝と夜は寒くて、昼は暑いもんね
Mornings and evenings are cold, but it gets hot during the day.

お大事に!
Take care!

ありがとう
Thanks.

105

Breakfast

おはよー
Good morning.

起きる時間だよ！
It's time to wake up!

ううん...わかったー
Yeah, got it.

まだ眠たい？
Are you still sleepy?

うん
Yeah.

ハハっ
Haha.

顔洗っておいで！
Go to wash your face!

はーい..
Okay..

朝ごはんできてるよ
Breakfast is ready.

うん！
Yeah.

でも先に着替えておいで
But change your clothes first.

今日はパンと目玉焼きだよ
Today, we have bread and fried egg.

うん、ありがとう
Okay, thanks.

ジャムいる？
Do you want jam?

うん
Yeah.

ケチャップもいる
Ketchup too.

106

はい はい
Okay okay.

なに の
何 飲みたい？
What do you want to drink?

うん
Okay.

きょう きゅうしょく なに
今日の給食は何かなぁ
I wonder what's for lunch today.

オレンジジュース
Orange juice.

ハハハハ
Hahaha.

ごちそうさまでした
Thank you for the meal.

きゅうしょく こと かんが
もう給食の事を考えてるの？
Are you already thinking about lunch?

がっこう じゅんび
学校の準備できてる？
Are you ready for school?

へへ
Hehe.

うん
Yeah.

じゃあ き
じゃあ気をつけてね
Alright, be careful.

きょう たいいく
今日は体育があったね
You have a PE class today, right?

い
行ってきます
I'm off.

たいそうふく も
体操服持った？
Did you take your gym clothes?

い
行ってらっしゃい
Have a good day.

うん
Yeah.

きょう いちにちがんば
今日も一日頑張ってね！
Good luck for another day today!

107

早<ruby>く<rt>はや</rt></ruby>着替<ruby>えないと・・・<rt>きが</rt></ruby>

早く着替えないと・・・
Oh, I have to change clothes quickly.

昨日、早く寝なかったからでしょ
That's because you didn't go to bed early last night.

寝過ごしちゃった
I overslept.

今日は何しようかな
I wonder what should I do today.

起きれなかった
I couldn't wake up.

朝ごはん、食べる?
Are you having breakfast?

何で起こしてくれなかったの?
Why didn't you wake me up?

昨日、何時に寝たの?
What time did you go to sleep yesterday?

目覚ましかけてなかったの?
Didn't you put your alarm on?

今日はいつもより早く起きた
I got up earlier than usual today.

あまり時間ない
I don't have much time.

忘れ物ない?
Did you forget anything?

急がないといけない
I need to hurry.

何時に帰ってくる?
What time will you be back?

今日の予定は?
What's your plan for today?

お弁当忘れないで
Don't forget your bento.

108

ただいまー
I'm back.

シバくん元気そうだった？
Is Shiba-kun doing well?

おかえりー
Welcome back.

今日はどんな一日だった？
How was your day today?

うん！全然変わってなかったよ
Yeah, he's doing fine! He hasn't changed much at all.

また会う約束した
We made plans to meet up again.

まぁまぁ
It was okay

よかったじゃん
That's wonderful!

今日、久しぶりにシバくんに会った
Today, I met Shiba-kun after a long time.

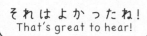

会えて嬉しかったよ
I was really happy to see him.

今日は疲れたからもう寝る
I'm feeling tired today,
so I'm going to bed now.

それはよかったね！
That's great to hear!

そう！おやすみ！
I see. Goodnight!

うん！おやすみー！
Yeah! Goodnight!

109

お風呂入るよー
Let's take a bath.

つぎ からだ あら
次は体を洗うよー
Next I'm going to wash your body.

は ー い
Yes.

うん
Yeah.

ふくぬ
服脱げる?
Can you take off your clothes?

きれい
綺麗になったね
You are clean now.

うん
Yeah.

ママ、ありがとう
Thank you mom.

さき あ
先にシャワー浴びよう
Let's take a shower first.

ふろ はい
お風呂入っていいよ
You can take a bath now.

かみ あら
髪、洗おっか
Let's wash your hair.

からだあら
ママ、体洗うから
I'm going to wash my body.

オッケー
Okay.

うん
Yeah.

シャンプーするよー
Shampooing.

ママ、まだー?
Mom, are you done yet?

もうすぐ
Soon.

110

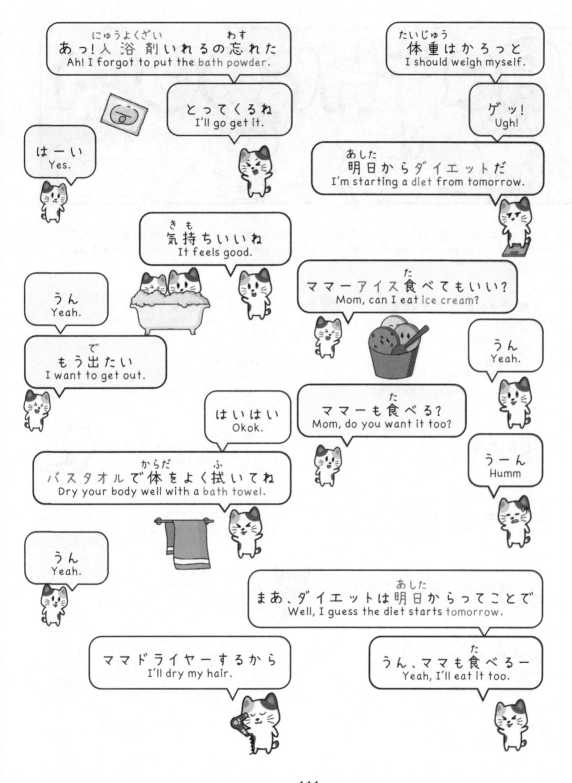

あっ!入浴剤いれるの忘れた
Ah! I forgot to put the bath powder.

体重はかろっと
I should weigh myself.

とってくるね
I'll go get it.

ゲッ!
Ugh!

はーい
Yes.

明日からダイエットだ
I'm starting a diet from tomorrow.

気持ちいいね
It feels good.

ママーアイス食べてもいい?
Mom, can I eat ice cream?

うん
Yeah.

うん
Yeah.

もう出たい
I want to get out.

ママーも食べる?
Mom, do you want it too?

はいはい
Okok.

うーん
Humm

バスタオルで体をよく拭いてね
Dry your body well with a bath towel.

うん
Yeah.

まあ、ダイエットは明日からってことで
Well, I guess the diet starts tomorrow.

ママドライヤーするから
I'll dry my hair.

うん、ママも食べるー
Yeah, I'll eat it too.

111

家に帰って来たら、手を洗ってね
When you get home, wash your hands.

バスタオルで、体を拭いてね
Use the bath towel to dry your body.

歯磨き粉とってくれる？
Can you get the toothpaste, please?

爪を切らなくちゃ
I need to cut my nails.

髪、洗った？
Did you wash your hair?

早く顔を洗っておいで
Hurry up and wash your face.

髪をとかさないとボサボサのままだよ
If you don't comb your hair, it stays messy.

髭を剃ってるの？
Are you shaving?

髪を乾かさないと風邪ひくよ
You'll catch a cold if you don't dry your hair.

化粧をしてるところだよ
I'm in the middle of putting on makeup.

シャワーを浴びてるところだよ
I'm taking a shower right now.

歯磨きした？
Did you brush your teeth?

お風呂に入りたい気分
I feel like I want to take a bath.

体重を量ろう
Let's check my weight.

温かいお風呂にゆっくり浸りたい
I want to soak leisurely in a warm bath.

ボディークリームを塗る
I apply body cream.

112

何してるの？
What are you doing?

メイクしてる
I'm doing my makeup.

どこか行くの？
Going somewhere?

うん
Yeah.

何時くらいに帰って来るの？
What time do you think you'll be back?

わからない
I don't know.

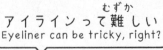

アイラインって難しい
Eyeliner can be tricky, right?

そうだよね
Yeah, it can be.

リキッドアイライナー使うと簡単だよ
Using liquid eyeliner makes it easier, you know.

うん
Yeah.

このシャドーとこのリップの色合うと思う？
Do you think this eyeshadow goes well with this lipstick color?

うん、合うと思うよ
Yeah, I think they go well together.

ねぇ、パウダー使っていい？
Hey, can I use some powder?

その化粧箱に入ってるよ
It's in that makeup box.

113

ねぇ、何みてるの?
Hey, what are you watching?

あと、台所の電気も消して
and turn off the light in the kitchen.

アニメ
Cartoon.

はいはい
Yes yes.

一緒にみる?
Do you wanna watch together?

やっぱり、映画みよー
Actually, let's watch a movie.

うん
Yeah.

あーなんか暑いなぁ
It's kinda hot here.

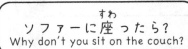
ソファーに座ったら?
Why don't you sit on the couch?

窓開けてー
Can you open the window?

うん
Yeah.

扇風機もつけてー
Can you turn on the fan too?

ねぇ、もう座っていい?
Hey, can I sit down now?

その前にリモコンとって
But first, pass me the remote control.

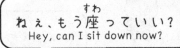

どこにあるの?
Where is it?

あっ!ポップコーン
Ah! popcorns.

もう自分でやって!
Do it yourself!

テーブルの上
On the table.

114

テレビをつけます
I turn on the TV.

しょくぶつ　みず
植物に水をやります
I water the plants.

テレビを消します
け
I turn off the TV.

テレビをみてるけどつまらない
I'm watching TV, but it's boring.

でんき
電気をつけます
I turn on the light.

ほん　よ
本を読んでいます
I'm reading a book.

でんき　け
電気を消します
I turn off the light.

ひるね
昼寝をしようかな
I think I'll take a nap

でんわ
電話をかけます
I make a phone call.

すこ きゅうけい
少し休憩します
I'm going to take a short break.

すわ
ソファーに座ります
I sit on the couch.

けいたい　さが
ネコちゃんは携帯を探しています
Neko-chan is looking for a cell phone.

まど　あ
窓を開けてください
Please open the window.

きょう　いえ
今日は家にいようかな
I think I'll stay at home today.

まど　し
窓を閉めます
I close the window.

カーテンを吊るしました
つ
I hung the curtains.

115

Dinner

ねぇ、今日何食べたい?
Hey, what do you want to eat today?

うーん、なんでもいい
Hmm, anything is fine.

でた!"なんでもいい"
There you go again!
"Anything is fine."

毎日メニュー考えるの大変なんだから
It's tough coming up with a menu every day.

食べたいもの言ってよ・・・
Just tell me what you want to eat・・・

うーん、そうだなぁ
Hmm

唐揚げ?
Fried chicken?

唐揚げなら材料ある
Fried chicken sounds good,
We have the ingredients.

オッケー
Ok

まず、ご飯を炊いて
First, cook the rice,

それから鶏肉の下味をつけて
then marinate the chicken,

下準備完了
Preparation is done.

サラダも作ろうかな
I should make a salad too.

レタスとトマトと・・・たまご
Lettuce, tomatoes, and...egg

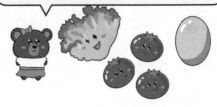

116

さいご　とりにく　あ
最後に鶏肉を揚げて
At last, fry the chicken,

よしっ!できた
Yes! done.

はん
ご飯できたよー!
Dinner is ready!

はーい
Yees.

うわっ!うまそう
Wow! Looks delicious.

いただきます
Let's dig in.

いただきます
Let's dig in.

あっ!しお
あっ!塩とって
Ah! pass me the salt.

はい
Here you go.

きょう　おそ
今日パパ遅くなるって
Dad said he'll be home late today.

そうなんだ
I see.

きょうがっこう
今日学校どうだったの?
How was school today?

ふつう
普通
Just normal.

もうすぐテストじゃないの?
Aren't your exams coming up soon?

うん
Yeah.

あと　べんきょう
後で、勉強する
I'll study later.

なに
何してるの?
What are you doing?

ゲーム
Playing a game.

べんきょう
勉強するんじゃなかった?
Weren't you supposed to study?

あと
後でする
I'll do it later.

ぜったい
絶対しないな・・こりゃ・・
I doubt you will...

Zzz

オーブントースターでパンを焼いたよ
I toasted bread in the toaster oven.

シチューを二十分煮込むよ
I will simmer the stew for twenty minutes.

炊飯器でご飯を炊いてくれる？
Can you cook rice in the rice coooker?

卵と小麦粉を混ぜて
Mix the eggs and flour.

電子レンジでご飯を温めよう
Let's heat up rice in the microwave.

海老を揚げたい
I want to deep fry the shrimps.

包丁で野菜を切って
Cut vegetables with a knife.

先に魚を焼こう
Let's grill the fish first.

玉ねぎは細かく切ってね
Cut onions into small pieces.

クリームはもう泡立てたの？
Have you already whipped the cream?

鍋でブロッコリーを茹でたらいい？
Should I boil broccoli in a pot?

きゅうりを薄く切ってね
Please thinly slice the cucumber.

林檎の皮を剥いたよ
I peeled apples.

野菜は蒸したほうがヘルシーだよ
Steaming vegetables is healthier.

もう野菜を炒めた？
Have you stir-fried the vegetables yet?

肉を焦がしてしまった
I accidentally burned the meat.

cleaning

部屋の掃除をしよう！
Let's clean the room!

今日は部屋の片付けをしたよ
I cleaned up my room today.

後で掃除機をかけてね！
Vacuum up later!

ワニくんの部屋は汚い
Wani-kun's room is messy.

床をほうきで掃いてくれる？
Can you sweep the floor?

服が汚れちゃった
My clothes got dirty.

天気がいいので洗濯物を干した
I hung up the laundry because the weather was nice.

テーブルを拭いた
I wiped the table.

アイロンを使ってもいい？
Can I use the iron?

床をモップで拭いた
I mopped the floor.

部屋の換気をした方がいいよ
It's better to ventilate the room.

服を畳んでくれる？
Can you fold the clothes?

鏡をピカピカに磨いた
I polished the mirror until it was sparkling.

本棚の埃をとって
Dust off the bookshelf.

服にシミがついてるよ
There's a stain on your clothes.

食器を洗った
I washed the dishes.

cleaning

今日たくさん掃除する場所あるから
I have a lot of places to clean today,

次、何すればいい？
What should I do next?

掃除手伝ってくれる？
Can you help me with the cleaning?

うん、いいよー
Sure.

じゃあゴミを出してきてくれる？
Can you take the trash out for me?

何すればいい？
What should I do?

うん、いいよー
Sure.

私、玄関の掃除するね
I'll clean the entrance area.

この部屋の掃除機かけてくれる？
Can you vacuum this room?

出してきたよー
Trash is out.

オッケー
Okay.

ありがとう
Thank you.

私は洗濯物を干すから
I'll hang out the laundry.

次、何すればいい？
What should I do next?

掃除機かけ終わったよ
I'm done vacuuming.

食器を洗ってくれる？
しょっき　あら
Can you wash the dishes?

でき たよー
It's done.

うん
Yeah.

わー！ピカピカになったね！
Wow! they're sparkling now!

洗剤、もうすぐなくなるよー
せんざい
The dish soap is running low.

ありがとう
Thank you.

まだ すること ある？
Is there anything else to do?

台所の下の棚に新しいのがあるよー
だいどころ　した　たな　あたら
There's a new one under the kitchen sink.

オッケー
Okay.

ううん、あとはもういいよ
Nah, we're good now.

次、何すればいい？
つぎ　なに
What should I do next?

手伝ってくれてありがとう
てつだ
Thank you for your help.

窓を拭いてくれる？
まど　ふ
Can you wipe the windows?

全然大丈夫
ぜんぜんだいじょうぶ
No problem.

うん
Yeah.

窓を拭く雑巾ある？
まど　ふ　ぞうきん
Do you have the cloth to
clean the windows?

掃除した後は気持ちいいね
そうじ　　あと　きも
After cleaning, everything feels so much
better, doesn't it?

綺麗になった！
きれい
Wow, they're sparkling now!

お風呂場に雑巾とバケツがある
ふろば　ぞうきん
There's a cloth and a bucket in the
bathroom.

完璧だね
かんぺき
It's perfect

うん、そうだね
Yeah, definitely.

 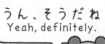

は ー い！席について
<ruby>席<rt>せき</rt></ruby>
Alright, everyone,
take your seats.

今日は昨日のテストを返します
<ruby>今日<rt>きょう</rt></ruby> <ruby>昨日<rt>きのう</rt></ruby> <ruby>返<rt>かえ</rt></ruby>
Today, I'll be returning yesterday's test.

うわー緊張する
<ruby>緊張<rt>きんちょう</rt></ruby>
Oh boy, I'm nervous.

私、全然自信ない・・・
<ruby>私<rt>わたし</rt>全然自信<rt>ぜんぜんじしん</rt></ruby>
I really don't have much
confidence in this one.

僕も・・・
<ruby>僕<rt>ぼく</rt></ruby>
Me neither.

難しかったです・・・
<ruby>難<rt>むずか</rt></ruby>
It was quite challenging・・・

そうですね
Yes, indeed.

今回のテストは難しかったと思います
<ruby>今回<rt>こんかい</rt></ruby> <ruby>難<rt>むずか</rt></ruby> <ruby>思<rt>おも</rt></ruby>
I think this test was quite difficult.

名前を呼ぶので取りに来てください
<ruby>名前<rt>なまえ</rt> <rt>よ</rt></ruby> <ruby>取<rt>と</rt></ruby> <ruby>来<rt>き</rt></ruby>
I'll call your names,
so please come up to collect your test.

はい
Yes.

シカちゃん
Shika-chan

はい
Yes.

カッパくん
Kappa-kun

シカちゃんどうだった？
How did you do, Shika-chan?

六十点
<ruby>六十点<rt>ろくじゅってん</rt></ruby>
I got 60 points.

僕五十五点だった・・・
<ruby>僕五十五点<rt>ぼくごじゅうごてん</rt></ruby>
I only got 55.

みなさん、テストは返ってきましたか？
Have you all recieved your test results?

では、授業を始めます
Alright then, let's begin the lesson.

はーい・・・
Yees...

教科書三十ページを見てください
Please look at page thirty of the textbook.

シカちゃん、文を読んでください
Shika-chan, please read the sentence.

今回の平均点は五十六点でした
The average score for this test was 56 points.

はい
Yes.

ふぅー
Phew

はい、では次カッパくん
Alright, next, Kappa-kun,

平均点も低かったんだね
the average is pretty low too, huh?

続きを読んでください
please continue from where Shika-chan left off.

うん、よかったー
Yeah, that's a relief.

はい
Yes.

ありがとうございます
Thank you.

間違えたところを
the questions where you made mistakes

時間がないので
We're running out of time,

よく見直しておいてください
Please review carefully.

この問題は宿題にします
so I'll assign this question as homework.

はーい・・・
Yes

次の授業までにやってきてください
Please have it done by the next class.

123

こんにちは
Hello.

ネコちゃんいますか？
Is Neko-chan here?

しゅくだいも
宿題持ってきたよ
I brought my homework.

シカちゃん
Shika-chan.

はい、いるよー
Yes, she is here.

どうぞ、あがって
Please come in.

うん！一緒にやろう
Great! Let's do it together.

じゃま
お邪魔します
Thank you for having me.

にかい
ネコちゃん二階にいるよ
Neko-chan is upstairs.

きょう さんすう こくご しゅくだい
今日は算数と国語の宿題があるね
We have math and Japanese homework today.

うん
Yeah.

はい
Okay.

はや しゅくだいお あそ
早く宿題終わらせて遊ぼう
Let's finish our homework quickly
and then play.

ネコちゃん
Neko-chan.

うん、そうだね！
Sounds good!

この問題シカちゃんわかる？
Do you get it this question, Shika-chan?

もうすぐ終わる
I'm almost done.

えっ！どれ？
Huh? Which one?

私も
Me too.

うーん
Um...

コンコン

たしか今日授業でやったやつだよね
I think we covered this one in class today, right?

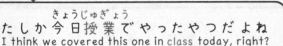

うん
Yeah.

ジュースとおやつ持ってきたよ
I brought juice and sweets.

これ難しいね
This one's quite challenging.

わーい
Yay.

だよね
I know, right?

宿題頑張ってるね
You guys are working hard on your homework.

教科書みてみよ
Let's check the textbook.

うん
Yep

あっここに書いてる
Oh, it's explained here.

終わったらシカちゃんと公園に遊びに行く
When we finish, we go to the park and play.

あー、こうやって解くんだ
Ah, that's how to solve it.

外、暑いから帽子かぶっていってね！
It's hot outside so wear a hat!

125

しょうがっこう　にゅうがく
ネコちゃんは小学校に入学します
Neko-chan enter elementary school.

わたし　しょうがくせい
私は小学生です
I'm an elementary student.

しがつ　にゅうがくしき
四月に入学式があります
There is an entrance ceremony in April.

わたし　ちゅうがくせい
私は中学生です
I'm a junior high school student.

ちゅうがっこう　そつぎょう
シバくんは中学校を卒業します
Shiba-kun is graduating from junior high school.

わたし　こうこうせい
私は高校生です
I'm a high school student.

さんがつ　そつぎょうしき
三月に卒業式があります
There is a graduation ceremony in March.

わたし　だいがくせい
私は大学生です
I'm a college student.

がっこう　い　まえ　せいふく　き
学校に行く前に制服を着ます
I put on the uniform before going to school.

がっこう　い
学校に行きます
I'm going to school.

にほん　がっこう　せいと　うわば　は
日本の学校では生徒は上履きを履きます
In Japanese school, students wear indoor shoes.

たいそうふく　わす
体操服を忘れました
I forgot my gym clothes.

えいご　べんきょう
ネコちゃんは英語を勉強します
Neko-chan study English.

じゅぎょうちゅう　ねむ
授業中ずっと眠たかった
I was sleepy the whole class.

きょう　しゅくだい
今日はたくさん宿題があります
I have lots of homework today.

らいしゅう
来週、テストがあります
I have a test next week.

computer

パソコンの電源を入れてください
Please turn on the computer.

携帯を充電しないと
I need to charge my phone.

パスワードは何ですか?
What's the password?

メールに画像を添付しました
I have attached the image to the e-mail.

メールを送りましたか?
Did you send an e-mail?

パソコンを再起動したほうがいいですね
It's better restart the computer.

メールの返信をしたいです
I'd like to reply to the e-mail.

この画像をダウンロードしたいです
I want to download this image.

このメールを転送してください
Please forward this email.

パソコンの画面が割れています
My computer screen is broken.

書類を印刷しました
I printed the documents.

インターネットに接続できません
I can't connect to the internet.

写真を保存してください
Please save the photos.

パソコンの電源を切ってもいいですか?
Can I turn off the computer?

このファイルを削除してください
Please delete this file.

マウスが壊れました
My mouse is broken.

127

かいぎ　はじ
会議を始めます
Let's begin the meeting.

ぜんかい　　　　　　　あじ　こうひょう
前回のトマト味は好評でした
The tomato flavor from the previous time was well-received.

しっ　あつ
ミーティング室に集まってください
Please gather in the conference room.

あたら　あじ
新しい味のアイディアはありますか？
Do you have any ideas for new flavors?

はい
Yes

はい
Yes.

きょう　しんしょうひん　　　　　　はな　あ
今日は新商品について話し合います
Today, we'll be discussing our new products.

のり
わさび海苔はどうでしょうか？
How about wasabi seaweed flavor?

しりょう　くば
資料を配ります
I'll pass out the documents.

よさそうですね
That sounds interesting.

しりょう
では資料2ページをみてください
Please look at page two of the documents.

しょうゆ
醤油はどうでしょうか？
What about soy sauce flavor?

あたら　あじ
まずは、ポテトチップスの新しい味について
First, let's talk about our new potato chip flavors.

あじ
コーラ味は？
How about cola flavor?

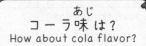

コーラ<ruby>味<rt>あじ</rt></ruby>・・・
Cola flavor...

<ruby>斬新<rt>ざんしん</rt></ruby>ですね
that's quite unique.

シカさん
Shika-san

プロジェクトのチームを<ruby>作<rt>つく</rt></ruby>ってください
can you assemble a team for this project?

<ruby>他<rt>ほか</rt></ruby>には？
Any other suggestions?

はい
Of course

<ruby>市場調査<rt>しじょうちょうさ</rt></ruby>も<ruby>次<rt>つぎ</rt></ruby>までに<ruby>願<rt>ねが</rt></ruby>お願いします
And please do market research by the next meeting.

<ruby>梅塩味<rt>うめしおあじ</rt></ruby>とか
Plum and salt flavor...

はい
Yes

カレー<ruby>味<rt>あじ</rt></ruby>はどうでしょう？
How about curry flavor?

よろしくお<ruby>願<rt>ねが</rt></ruby>いします
Thank you

どれも<ruby>試食<rt>ししょく</rt></ruby>してみないと<ruby>想像<rt>そうぞう</rt></ruby>できないな
I can't really imagine how they'd taste without trying them.

<ruby>次<rt>つぎ</rt></ruby>のミーティングまでに<ruby>試食<rt>ししょく</rt></ruby>の<ruby>用意<rt>ようい</rt></ruby>を<ruby>願<rt>ねが</rt></ruby>お願いします
Please prepare samples for tasting by the next meeting.

はい
Yes

お電話ありがとうございます
（でんわ）
Thank you for calling.

少々お待ちください
（しょうしょう ま）
Just a moment, please.

ドッグカンパニーのシバです
This is Shiba speaking from Dog Company.

ありがとうございます
Thank you very much.

お待たせいたしました
（ま）
Thank you for holding.

お世話になっております
（せわ）
Thank you for your assistance.

ブルです
This is Bull.

キャットカンパニーのネコです
This is Neko from Cat Company.

ブルさんはいらっしゃいますでしょうか？
May I speak to Bull-san, please?

あっ!間違えて切ってしまった..
（まちが き）
Oops! I hung up by mistake...

ブルに電話をお繋ぎします
（でんわ つな）
Let me connect you to Bull.

あれっ?もしもーし?
Hello? Hello?

130

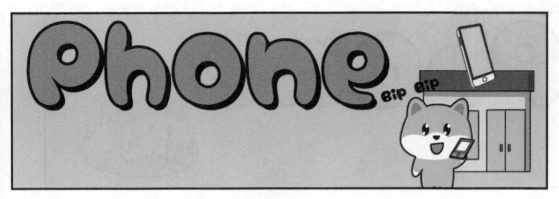

~さんはいらっしゃいますか
May I speak to ~san?

~していただけますか？
Would you mind ~ ing?

ようけん　うかが
ご用件をお伺いします
How can I help you?

もう　わけ
申し訳ございませんが～
I'm sorry but~

き
聞こえますか？
Can you hear me?

なまえ　　　うかが
お名前をお伺いしてもよろしいですか？
May I have your name, please?

でんわ　　　つな
電話をお繋ぎします
I'll put you through.

でんごん　　　あず
伝言をお預かりしましょうか？
Could I take a message?

あと　　　なお
また後でかけ直します
I'll call back later.

いちどい
もう一度言っていただけますか？
Could you say that again?

がいしゅつ
ただいま外出しております
He is out at the moment.

れんらく　　　　　　　　　　つた
ご連絡があったことをお伝えいたします
I let (him or her) know that you called.

でんわ
電話してください
Call me please.

でんわ
お電話ありがとうございました
Thank you for your calling.

ほか　　　ようけん
他にご用件はございますか？
Can I help you with anything else?

しつれい
失礼いたします
This phrase is used when hung up the phone.

131

phone

もしもし
Hello.

もしもし
Hello.

今日は 誕生日会 行けなくてごめんね
Sorry I can't make it to your birthday party today.

ぜんぜんき
全然気にしないで
Don't worry about it at all.

たんじょうび
ネコちゃんお誕生日おめでとう
Happy birthday Neko-chan.

きょう　　　しごとおそ
今日は仕事遅くなるから
I'll be working late today.

あっ!シバくんありがとう
Shiba-kun Thank you.

こんど あ　　とき　　　　　　　わた
今度会った時にプレゼント渡すね
I'll give you a present when we meet next time.

こえ　　き
声が聞きたくて
I wanted to hear your voice,

ありがとう
Thanks.

でんわ
電話しちゃった
so I called.

うれ
嬉しい!ありがとう!
I'm glad you did! Thanks!

さいきん　　　　　　　　あ
最近なかなか 会えてないもんね
We haven't been able to meet up much lately.

うん
Yeah.

132

お互い忙しいもんね
both of us have been busy.

でも来月はけっこう暇だよ
But I have quite a bit of free time next month.

あ！そうなの？
Oh! Do you?

じゃあ来月会おうよ
Let's plan to meet next month then.

そうだね
Sure.

また空いてる日連絡するね
I'll let you know when I have free days.

うん
Yeah

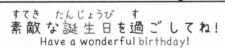

じゃあ今日は思いっきり楽しんでね
Well, enjoy your day to the fullest today.

素敵な誕生日を過ごしてね！
Have a wonderful birthday!

うん
Yeah.

わざわざ電話してくれてありがとう
Thank you for calling me.

うん
Yeah.

じゃあ、またね
Okay then, talk to you later.

うん、バイバイ
Sure, Bye.

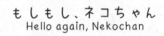
A few hours later

もしもし、ネコちゃん
Hello again, Nekochan

今日、誕生日会行けるよー
I can go to your birthday party today.

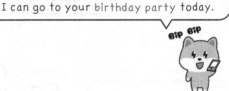
gip gip

嬉しい！じゃあ待ってるね
I'm so happy, I'll be waiting for you.

お誕生日おめでとうネコちゃん
Happy birthday Neko-chan

133

Video Game

よーい、スタート
Ready, set, go!

シバくん行くよー！
Let's go Shiba-kun!

うん！
Yeah

僕が勝つよ
I'm going to win.

いやっ、負けないよ
Oh, no you won't.

シバくん、ドリフト上手いね
You're good at drifting, Shiba-kun.

へへへ
Hehehe

いっぱい練習したからね
I practiced a lot.

ほいっ！バナナの皮
Banana peel for you!

うわっ！追い越された
Oh no, I got overtaken.

イカスミ攻撃だ！
Squid ink attack!

うわっ！前が見えない
I can't see anything ahead.

よしっ！このままゴールだ
Alright, I'm going to make it to the finish line.

うわー負けたー
Oh, I lost.

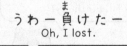

次は勝つぞ！
I will win next time!

Video Game

ぶき さが
武器を探さないといけない
I need to search for weapons.

どんなアイテム 持ってるの?
も
What items do you have?

かれ ひっさつわざ
あれは彼の必殺技だよ
That's his special move.

かきん
課金しないとプレイできないんだ
I have to make in-game purchases to play.

いっしょ
一緒にゲームしよ
Let's play the video game together.

そくし
即死しちゃった
I got instantly killed.

ちず み
地図を見つけた
I found the map.

たお
ラスボスを倒したよ
I defeated the final boss.

お つ
落ち着いて
Stay calm.

かく
隠れろ
Hide.

てき つよ
あの敵は強かった
That enemy was tough.

き
気をつけて
Watch out.

ちかみち
こっちが近道だよ
This way is a shortcut.

てき ちか
敵が近くにいるよ
Enemies are nearby.

セーブした?
Did you save?

りょうかい
了解
Got it.

135

ROMAJI

A	I	U	E	O
あ ア	い イ	う ウ	え エ	お オ
Ka か カ	**Ki** き キ	**Ku** く ク	**Ke** け ケ	**Ko** こ コ
Sa さ サ	**Shi** し シ	**Su** す ス	**Se** せ セ	**So** そ ソ
Ta た タ	**Chi** ち チ	**Tsu** つ ツ	**Te** て テ	**To** と ト
Na な ナ	**Ni** に ニ	**Nu** ぬ ヌ	**Ne** ね ネ	**No** の ノ
Ha は ハ	**Hi** ひ ヒ	**Fu** ふ フ	**He** へ ヘ	**Ho** ほ ホ
Ma ま マ	**Mi** み ミ	**Mu** む ム	**Me** め メ	**Mo** も モ
Ya や ヤ		**Yu** ゆ ユ		**Yo** よ ヨ
Ra ら ラ	**Ri** り リ	**Ru** る ル	**Re** れ レ	**Ro** ろ ロ
Wa わ ワ		**O** を ヲ		**N** ん ン

Ga がガ	**Gi** ぎギ	**GU** ぐグ	**Ge** げゲ	**Go** ごゴ
Za ざザ	**Ji** じジ	**Zu** ずズ	**Ze** ぜゼ	**Zo** ぞゾ
Da だダ	**Ji** ぢヂ	**Zu** づヅ	**De** でデ	**Do** どド
Ba ばバ	**Bi** びビ	**Bu** ぶブ	**Be** べベ	**Bo** ぼボ
Pa ぱパ	**Pi** ぴピ	**Pu** ぷプ	**Pe** ぺペ	**Po** ぽポ

Kya きゃキャ	**Kyu** きゅキュ	**Kyo** きょキョ	**Gya** ぎゃギャ	**Gyu** ぎゅギュ	**Gyo** ぎょギョ
Sha しゃシャ	**Shu** しゅシュ	**Sho** しょショ	**Ja** じゃジャ	**Ju** じゅジュ	**Jo** じょジョ
Cha ちゃチャ	**Chu** ちゅチュ	**Cho** ちょチョ	**Ja** ぢゃヂャ	**Ju** ぢゅヂュ	**Jo** ぢょヂョ
Nya にゃニャ	**Nyu** にゅニュ	**Nyo** にょニョ	**Hya** ひゃヒャ	**Hyu** ひゅヒュ	**Hyo** ひょヒョ
Bya びゃビャ	**Byu** びゅビュ	**Byo** びょビョ	**Pya** ぴゃピャ	**Pyu** ぴゅピュ	**Pyo** ぴょピョ
Mya みゃミャ	**Myu** みゅミュ	**Myo** みょミョ	**Rya** りゃリャ	**Ryu** りゅリュ	**Ryo** りょリョ

Made in the USA
Las Vegas, NV
12 January 2024

84251977R10077